Adult Children of Alcoholic Parents

This workbook belongs to:

_____

Adult Children of Alcoholic Parents

An Evidence-Based Workbook to Heal Your Past

Kara Lissy, LCSW

ROCKRIDGE
PRESS

For general information on our other products and services or to obtain technical support, please contact our Customer Care Department within the United States at (866) 744-2665, or outside the United States at (510) 253-0500.

Rockridge Press publishes its books in a variety of electronic and print formats. Some content that appears in print may not be available in electronic books, and vice versa.

Interior and Cover Designer: Erin Yeung
Art Producer: Janice Ackerman
Editor: Jed Bickman
Production Editor: Matthew Burnett
Production Manager: Jose Olivera

Illustration: © 2021 Geometrica Bureau/Creative Market
Author photo: Alyssa Peek, Peek Photography

ISBN: Print 978-1-64876-813-2
eBook 978-1-64876-239-0

R0

Thank you…

Michael: *For my motivation*
Mom and Pete: *For my determination*
Dad: *For my inspiration; I miss you every day.*

Contents

Introduction

Welcome to this workbook for adult children of alcoholics. My name is Kara, and it is a great honor to walk alongside you as you learn, grow, and heal. I've walked through the recovery steps in this book on my own. I respect you for picking up this book. As a licensed clinical social worker and psychotherapist, I've had the privilege of working with adult children from alcoholic or otherwise dysfunctional homes. I've witnessed firsthand the strength, resilience, and growth that are uncovered by doing this important work together.

Opening yourself to the vulnerabilities of self-discovery is an act of true courage, so I congratulate you for taking this first step!

As you begin this journey, which may seem daunting, please know you are not alone. The 2005 to 2010 National Surveys on Drug Use and Health reported that 7.5 million children lived with at least one parent with an alcohol use disorder. Combine that number with the adults who grew up with one or more alcoholic parents, and you have quite a large community beside you.

For the purposes of this book, I'll use the word "parent" to refer to any family member or caregiver involved in your upbringing. This book will still help even if you did not live in the same home as your alcoholic parent or if your parent got sober at some point during your childhood.

Many of you were drawn to this book because of difficulties communicating with family members, rigid or disrespected boundaries, or struggles with intimacy in other parts of your life. Perhaps you've found yourself in a painful déjà vu, repeating unhealthy patterns of behavior you observed in childhood. Or maybe you're feeling disconnected from your emotions or your sense of self. Whatever the reasons, you've landed in a safe place with this book. Little by little, we'll peel back layers of coping skills that no longer help so that you can discover your resilience and learn how to lead a life that allows you to be true to yourself and own every part of your story.

While this workbook can be completed alone, you don't have to go it alone. If you need more support, you may want to find a therapist who specializes in trauma. Therapists can be especially helpful when it comes to work on relationships and communication because they can provide real-time feedback and help you role-play scenarios.

This workbook is structured chronologically. In part 1, we'll take a look at your past and how you may have been affected by your family members' unhealthy behaviors and relationship to alcohol. This will provide context for how dysfunction from your childhood manifests itself today. It will also allow you to grieve for the aspects of a healthy childhood that you didn't have.

This paves the way for part 2, which focuses on issues related to yourself and others, including boundaries, communication, self-esteem, and intimacy. You'll learn specific skills to help you grow in these areas and develop more self-love in the process.

Part 3 will help you develop a blueprint for healthy relationships in the future. We'll examine what intimacy looks like in friendships, romantic relationships, and families of origin. You'll also learn what it means to develop intimacy with yourself.

This book is most effective if worked through from start to finish. Try to take your time as you complete the exercises; they'll help you deepen your connection to yourself. (All you need is your favorite pen, pencil, or marker to write with!) I hope the quotes, anecdotes, and vignettes sprinkled throughout the book will add some perspective.

Please know that while the journey might seem long, the prize of self-love is more than worth the effort. You can do this.

Let's begin with a short self-assessment to see where you are now.

How Has Alcohol Impacted Me?

This quiz contains some of the most common traits of an adult child of an alcoholic. Circle True or False for each statement and find the corresponding point values on page xi.

1. My relationships feel chaotic and full of drama. **True / False**

2. I'm good at sticking up for myself. **True / False**

3. Being vulnerable comes naturally to me. **True / False**

4. I struggle to stick up for myself when I'm being taken advantage of. **True / False**

5. I often feel disconnected from myself. **True / False**

6. It's easy for me to let people into my life. **True / False**

7. When someone lets me down, it's "one strike and you're out." **True / False**

8. I second-guess my decisions. **True / False**

9. It's hard for me to identify if I'm feeling angry and/or sad. **True / False**

10. I don't often think about being abandoned. **True / False**

11. I often find myself acting like a parent figure in my relationships. **True / False**

12. My romantic partners are emotionally available and know how to communicate. **True / False**

13. I have a hard time figuring out what's "normal" in social situations. **True / False**

Answer Key:

Tally up your points using the following key:

1. T = 0; F = 1
2. T = 0; F = 1
3. T = 1; F = 0
4. T = 1; F = 0
5. T = 0; F = 1
6. T = 1; F = 0
7. T = 1; F = 0
8. T = 1; F = 0
9. T = 0; F = 1
10. T = 1; F = 0
11. T = 0; F = 1
12. T = 1; F = 0
13. T = 1; F = 0

TOTAL:

A score of 4 or more indicates you've likely been affected by the alcoholic or otherwise dysfunctional behavior in your upbringing. In isolation, these questions may not seem to mean much, but together they build a pattern which is common of adult children of alcoholics.

Take a moment to reflect on the questions for which you received a point. How do these scenarios resonate with you? Jot down some notes here.

PART ONE

Healing the Past

In this part of the book, we'll examine the way early relationships shaped your view of the world, of others, and, most important, of yourself.

These anecdotes and exercises may bring up painful memories and reminders of your suffering, so it's crucial to approach them with curiosity, compassion, and care. As feelings rise to the surface, treat them without judgment as best you can. If this seems difficult when you feel overwhelmed, imagine you are gently listening to a close friend who has the feelings you are struggling with. Think about how you'd respond to them if painful feelings were to come up. Then, apply this same compassion to yourself.

Our pasts are a part of who we are and who we will become, but we no longer need to be victims. Once we learn that we cannot change the events that happened to us, we can change how we show up in the world today and tomorrow.

CHAPTER ONE

What It Means to Grow Up
in an Alcoholic Home

"A whole family is one in which each member can bring her full self to the table knowing that she will always be both held and free."

—GLENNON DOYLE, *UNTAMED*

If you look closely enough, each family has room for growth. Patterns of communication and parenting are passed down through generations; people learn to cope with their trauma differently. A mental illness or other ongoing stressor might also strain the parent-child dynamic.

As adult children of alcoholics, we faced a unique set of circumstances in childhood. These issues might present themselves at both ends of the same spectrum, with some having an exaggerated characteristic or behavior and others a complete absence of it. But the core struggles are largely the same for children of parents with alcoholism or other forms of dysfunction.

We may have not felt it was safe to honor our feelings or bring our true selves to the table. But that does not mean we are incapable of becoming whole ourselves and creating fulfilling lives of our own as adults.

Before embarking on that journey towards wholeness, we must first sharpen our understanding of alcohol dependence and how it manifests itself.

Starting with the Basics: Defining Alcohol Dependence

The term *alcoholic* is used to describe an individual struggling with an alcohol use disorder. The following terms, defined by the Diagnostic and Statistical Manual for Mental Disorders (DSM-5), are used to diagnose alcohol use disorder:

- Drinking greater quantities of alcohol, or drinking over a longer period of time, than you intended
- Trying to cut down on drinking but finding yourself unable to
- Spending a lot of time drinking or recovering from sickness as a result of drinking
- Experiencing cravings—a strong urge to drink
- Finding that drinking or being sick from drinking often interferes with taking care of your home or family; when your drinking causes issues with work or school performance
- Continuing to drink even though it is causing trouble with your family or friends
- Giving up or cutting back on activities that are important or fun in order to drink instead
- Getting into situations (more than once) where your chances of getting hurt are increased due to your drinking
- Continuing to drink even though it is making you feel depressed or anxious or adding to another health problem
- Having to drink much more than you previously did to get the effect you want
- Having withdrawal symptoms such as trouble sleeping, shakiness, irritability, anxiety, depression, restlessness, nausea, sweating, or hallucinations when alcohol is wearing off

Someone is said to have an alcohol use disorder when they meet at least two of these criteria for a period of 12 months or more. The severity of an alcohol use disorder is determined by how many of these criteria are met.

Alcoholism has many comorbidities, including, but not limited to, depression, anxiety, bipolar disorder, and PTSD. These illnesses can exacerbate each other in vicious cycles, so it's important to consider the possibility of alcohol or other substances as self-medication.

What It Means to Have Alcoholic Parents

Joscelyn's father is a high-powered executive. Although he's able to provide for their family and runs a successful company, on the weekends he drinks four or more drinks throughout the day and is quicker to anger at Joscelyn and her mother. Joscelyn feels she's walking on eggshells around him, although he rarely remembers his anger bursts the next day.

Dion's uncle Gabriel, who lives with him and his mother, got sober seven years ago when Dion was 10. Although Gabriel doesn't drink anymore, he doesn't contribute to the household. Instead of sticking up for herself, his mother keeps busy by cleaning, cooking, and doing all of Gabriel's laundry, which makes Dion resentful.

Although Joscelyn and Dion grew up in different circumstances, they overlap in some ways. For instance, both have observed difficulty with boundaries, assertiveness, and emotional expression. Both children are at risk of growing up with a core belief that their feelings don't matter or that they always have to be on high alert for conflict.

It's important to note from these stories that regardless of whether your parent is still actively drinking or not, they might still be engaging in dysfunctional patterns of behavior.

Similarly, an alcoholic may be able to function at work or home. Many people with alcohol use disorder might use this functional behavior to discredit others' concerns. For example, they may say, "If I were really an alcoholic, I'd have lost my job by now." Remember this does not absolve them of responsibility, nor does it invalidate your worry as a loved one.

You're Not Alone

Mia's family never talked openly about her father's alcoholism, and she grew up feeling ashamed of it. As an adult, she longs for deep connection, but her shame prevents her from opening up in her dating life.

Cameron's mother had a horrible temper when she used cocaine. He vowed to live a life free of the chaos he experienced as a child, and he now works meticulously at his job. To him, making a mistake is equivalent to failure.

Star's mother couldn't parent due to her alcohol use and has been in and out of inpatient treatment her whole life. As a young adult, Star has lost many friends because of her difficulty with trust. Once someone lets her down, even in a minor way, Star is quick to cut people out of her life with no explanation.

Although these stories are quite different, they share an important commonality: a feeling of being unsafe. It's important for caregivers to be a steady, reliable force in children's lives. When they are not, we cope with our shocked nervous system in several ways, such as:

- Refusing to be vulnerable with others
- Striving to be perfect
- Judging ourselves and others harshly
- Becoming preoccupied with relationships or friendships ending
- Surrounding ourselves with people whose behaviors resemble our parents'
- Rejecting others quickly before they can reject us first

If these coping strategies resonate with you, try not to judge yourself. The pain we experienced as children was simply too raw; we had to develop some form of protection. Perhaps these ways of coping have even helped you in your professional or personal life. In recovery, we have the power to choose which strategies we take with us and which we would like to leave behind.

What It Means to Be Part of a Dysfunctional Family

As a teenager, Akane prefers to keep a lot of her feelings to herself, especially about friendships and school. Her mother is concerned she doesn't know what's going on in her daughter's life, so she read her diary and humiliated Akane at the dinner table by sharing an entry with the whole family.

Conor's mother doesn't have many friends and often divulges too much detail about her dating and sexual life with Conor. He feels uncomfortable with these disclosures, but then feels guilty because he doesn't want to upset his mother or hurt her feelings.

A dysfunctional family is one in which conflict, misbehavior, disrespect, neglect, abuse, or domestic violence are common and continuous. This often leads children and other adult family members to overcompensate, either by enabling dysfunctional behavior, shutting down, or becoming hyper-responsible.

In alcoholic families specifically, there is a sense of emotional instability, unreliability, and difficulty with trust. Although alcoholic homes may not necessarily be abusive or neglectful, they are dysfunctional nonetheless, because the parent is often unable to regulate their own emotions or be present to validate the child's emotions. When a child is exposed to such mistreatment and emotional absence from a parent, it can lead to:

- Enabling
- Rigid expectations of self and others
- Conflict avoidance
- Inflexible boundaries or enmeshment
- Lack of assertiveness
- Exaggerated sense of self-importance (narcissism) or low self-esteem
- Manipulation, deceit, or intimidation
- Gaslighting
- Blaming others for one's own actions and feelings
- Codependence

Identifying Dysfunctional Behaviors

This quiz will help you get in touch with some common manifestations of growing up with a dysfunctional family. Circle True or False for each statement and find the corresponding point values below.

1. If someone lets me down, I'm more likely to cut them out of my life than forgive them. **True / False**

2. It's better to keep my mouth shut and avoid an argument than risk someone getting angry. **True / False**

3. I always take responsibility for my behavior. **True / False**

4. It's easy for me to stick up for myself. **True / False**

5. I don't share everything with my family. **True / False**

6. I often make excuses for, overlook, or clean up after my family member. **True / False**

7. I must feel needed by others in order to feel good about myself. **True / False**

8. I'm able to forgive myself when I make a mistake. **True / False**

9. I find myself making excuses for people when they treat me poorly. **True / False**

10. I frequently respond with rage when people disappoint me. **True / False**

Answer Key:

Give yourself the following points for these answers.

1. True = 1; False = 0
2. True = 1; False = 0
3. True = 0; False = 1
4. True = 0; False = 1
5. True = 0; False = 1
6. True = 1; False = 0
7. True = 1; False = 0
8. True = 0; False = 1
9. True = 1; False = 0
10. True = 1; False = 0

Six or more points indicate you have likely been affected by or exhibit dysfunctional behavior that you learned in childhood. Although this might make you feel overwhelmed, keep in mind that self-awareness is the first key step to making a positive change.

Emotional Abuse

Kiara's father places heavy emphasis on her academic performance and her achievements in figure skating. Whenever she comes home from school with a grade lower than an A, her father tells her she is worthless and scrutinizes every criticism from her teachers. His expression of love is dependent upon how much she succeeds in competitions and with her schoolwork.

Emotional abuse constitutes any behavior that threatens someone's psychological safety by making them feel bad about themselves. In dysfunctional families, this may look like:

- Name-calling
- Shaming (for example, weight/appearance, eating habits, school or athletic performance)
- Wrongfully blaming
- Twisting words
- Misuse of power to manipulate the child into doing or believing something
- Gaslighting
- Picking a favorite child and a scapegoat child
- Using a child to pass messages between parents, or one parent using a child to get back at another

At times, families can enter a vicious cycle between behavioral dysfunction, such as a teenager acting out, and emotional abuse, such as shaming the teen for their behavior.

Those of us who grew up with emotional abuse may experience trouble with assertiveness, a sense of disconnection from ourselves, and excessive people-pleasing behavior. We may unconsciously repeat the patterns we were exposed to by our parents by getting into friendships, intimate relationships, or toxic work environments that mimic these conditions. This is because we were never shown we deserved better.

Physical Abuse and Aggression

Physical abuse is any physical contact that threatens our safety or causes us bodily harm. Examples include, but are certainly not limited to, slapping, punching, pinching, shoving, bruising, and scratching.

Often, our parents were given faulty parenting skills and poor emotional regulation techniques from their parents. In fact, if we travel far enough back in history, we might find generations of abuse.

In your home, it's possible that parents were not the only ones who engaged in physical abuse; siblings or extended family members often also participate in these behaviors.

Physical abuse rarely acts alone. Emotional, verbal, and sexual abuse are sometimes coconspirators in this vicious, painful attempt to gain power and control over someone. If you grew up with an addicted parent, you may have learned to anticipate and associate abuse with your parents drinking or drug use and tried to "behave accordingly" to prevent it from happening.

Denial is often a powerful player in abuse dynamics as well. It might be even more common if the abuse occurred while your parent was intoxicated. Children may cover up for or try to protect their abuser, especially in cases where law enforcement or children services become involved.

As a survivor of abuse, you might struggle with sleep, appetite, and acts of physical affection. Management of your emotions might sway back and forth between completely shutting down and feeling overwhelmed by your feelings. Intimate relationships can become difficult due to issues with trust and vulnerability. Some survivors of abuse might feel disconnected from their bodies.

Neglect

Toni is eight years old and splits time between her parents. She's excited for a night of watching movies with her dad. But half an hour after arriving at his house, her father tells her he's going to a party. He tells her he will be back by 10 o'clock but doesn't come home until three in the morning. Toni spends most of her night hypervigilant, watching the window and checking to make sure the door is locked.

Neglect is a caregiver's failure to provide the resources necessary for a child's survival. It involves any action—or, more important, inaction—that might endanger a child's safety.

Because alcohol and substance abuse have mind-altering effects, it's not uncommon for neglect to follow close behind intoxication. Similarly, a parent might be neglectful if their mental illness causes significant impairments in their ability to provide care.

Emotional distancing is neglect's more subtle and frequently overlooked cousin. Parents who are emotionally distant might be able to provide basic needs such as food, clothing, and shelter but might remain detached in their attention and emotional responses. The emotionally distanced parent has trouble attuning to their child's emotional state, validating their feelings, and offering comfort in times of distress.

Authority figures, other parental figures, and even the adult child themselves might dismiss neglect because it doesn't always appear to cause active physical harm. It's easy to sweep neglect under the rug as no big deal. In the case of emotional distancing in particular, it's common to attribute a parent's emotional absence to part of their personality. The scars of neglect may not be overtly visible, but they are insidious in their own way and often manifest later in adulthood as attachment problems, difficulty identifying feelings, and trouble taking care of oneself.

Feelings and Needs Were Dismissed

Vinh was bullied badly in middle school. She'd come home in tears, often refusing to eat dinner and missing the bus the next day because of oversleeping. Vinh's mother did not want to get involved, claiming that her child was "being a typical preteen." Vinh eventually confided in her teacher that she no longer wanted to be alive. Concerned, the teacher phoned Vinh's mother to recommend that Vinh start seeing a therapist. Vinh's mother asked the teacher to stop calling, claiming that the situation was "under control" and that her daughter "just needed to grow some thick skin and get over it."

The journey from childhood to adolescence can be quite the bumpy ride. We're fraught with hormonal changes, intense feelings, and social competition with our peers. It's important to feel unconditionally loved and accepted. Steady parenting may not stop all of the pain, but it can help provide some security and comfort through the turbulence.

When we don't receive that comfort, we may slowly start to question whether our needs or feelings are important. This lack of comfort can come in the form of parents claiming we're over-reacting, displaying a blunted or complete lack of reaction when we verbalize frustration or sadness, or labeling us as needy or annoying.

Dysfunctional parents can make us feel as though our needs and feelings are great inconveniences. When we speak up, we often speak the truth, which may make others uncomfortable. As a result, we might learn to associate expression of our feelings with conflict and slowly stop expressing ourselves.

Parentification

Lucas is the oldest of four siblings. At times, his mother drinks so much she gets sick to her stomach and can't make it into work the next morning. Lucas has learned he cannot tell his mother to stop drinking without a violent argument, so he keeps a vigilant eye on how many beers she's had. This way, he can somewhat anticipate when it's time to get out the bucket and email his mother's boss that she'll be out the next day.

Parentification often looks like a role reversal between child and parent. Adult children might have to learn how to pay bills, take phone calls on behalf of the parent, care for a parent who's sick or hungover, or take care of younger siblings far beyond what's expected for their age.

This overexerted sense of responsibility is a powerful survival skill that can extend into adulthood. Parentified adult children have a difficult time distinguishing between their responsibility and others' and may frequently put others' needs ahead of their own to avoid conflict. In some cases, they might nitpick, nag, or try to control others' behaviors. They might also have a hard time relaxing and prioritizing self-care.

With parentification, control is an illusion. You might think that by taking responsibility for others' behaviors, you have control. But in fact, the only person you have control over is yourself. We'll circle back to this theme again in later sections.

Parenting styles are important in our recovery because they're closely tied to our attachment styles, which are typically divided into three categories: avoidant, anxious, and secure. Our parents are the first people we have contact with in the world, and through our relationship with them, we learn expectations for how other relationships should be. This, in turn, affects how we show up in our relationships as adolescents and adults.

Authoritarian parents place high value on obedience. They govern their households with discipline, rules, and structure. They tend to be strict and inflexible. Children of authoritarian parents are more likely to develop perfectionism and depression. Because adult children of authoritarian parents have become accustomed to harsh criticism, high standards, and strict punishment, they may develop an anxious or fearful attachment style. They might have received the message that love is contingent upon certain behaviors or expectations.

Authoritative parenting is characterized by consistent limit-setting and validation. Boundaries are firm but flexible, consequences appropriate for the scenario, and expectations clearly stated in terms children can understand. Adult children of authoritative parents grow up with a greater sense of self-efficacy and a secure attachment style. They are less likely to experience depression.

Permissive parents, as their title suggests, allow greater autonomy with their children but at the expense of modeling appropriate boundaries, consequences, and limit-setting. Without structure in their home, children of permissive parents may grow up to have an avoidant attachment style, characterized by a discomfort with emotional intimacy and closeness and a preoccupation with independence.

Uninvolved parents show little interest in their children's interests, activities, and habits. These parents often seem detached and preoccupied with their own lives. They offer little to no validation for positive behavior or consequences for undesirable behavior. Without consistent regulation of their emotions, children of these parents might also grow up with an avoidant attachment style.

Never Talking about It

Almost every time Cory's family drives home from a holiday, wedding, or other kind of party, his father gets sick from drinking too much and they have to pull the car over. Cory puts the pieces together that something isn't right with his father's behavior, but every time he asks his mother if everything is okay, she shrugs it off and tells him his father ate something bad, wasn't feeling well, or has a stomach virus. Cory always opts to go to his friends' houses instead of having friends over to his because he's not sure what kind of condition his father will be in.

Shame weaves a common thread through alcoholic and dysfunctional families. From the time we are young, our nervous systems are able to pick up that something about our family might be "different" from other families. The alcohol use, substance use, mental illness, or other form of abuse quickly becomes taboo, and we become indoctrinated into the unspoken order of "we just don't talk about that with others."

As we see with Cory's family, many children grow up hesitant to ask their parents about what is truly going on in their households because of the parents' own denial. It's important to remember denial is a powerful defense mechanism and coping skill for shame. At times, even our functional parent was unable to fully grasp or admit to themselves the severity of our alcoholic parent's behavior.

As a result, we learn, little by little, that sometimes it's better to keep our questions to ourselves. It becomes too painful to repeatedly expose ourselves to a lack of validation. We may even start to believe the denial, convincing ourselves that perhaps we're seeing things or making things up. Over time, this can lead to a continual denial of our own realities, a failure to speak up when we see wrongdoing, or a general mistrust of our feelings. Such bottling up of feelings can also lead to rage and resentment.

Chapter Wrap-Up

In this chapter, we've learned about the qualities of, and overlapping between, dysfunctional families and alcoholic families. Perhaps some of the text brought up painful memories or led you to examine you or your family's behavior in a new light. Such an understanding of how the past informs the present is crucial throughout our healing process. It is also the first step in acknowledging that, as children, we did not have control over the behavioral patterns, belief systems, and unhealthy ways of coping that preceded us; the things that happened to us were not our fault. And we certainly were not alone. You might notice that this first chapter doesn't include the exercises found in subsequent chapters; in part, that is because we can reflect on our past, but we can't change the past. Again, it wasn't your fault.

With this foundation, we can move forward with developing a more realistic view of the past, take responsibility for and heal from our own feelings, and learn how to utilize new coping skills in the future.

CHAPTER TWO

How Has Alcohol Affected Me?

"People cannot put traumatic events behind until they are able to acknowledge what has happened and start to recognize the invisible demons they're struggling with."

—BESSEL VAN DER KOLK, *THE BODY KEEPS THE SCORE*

Reading the previous section may have made you feel as though you are stuck in a perpetual struggle with themes from your childhood or adolescence. This is completely understandable. When our development is disrupted, it can feel difficult to see a way forward. That is where this next section comes in. Now that we've taken a look at what it means to grow up in an alcoholic or otherwise dysfunctional home, we are better able to take stock of our own individual pasts in a way that can help inform our approaches to the future. In this chapter, you'll find a variety of different exercises aimed at increasing your self-awareness, identifying key areas for improvement, and learning to recognize your strength and your resilience.

Taking Stock

When we take stock, we develop a deeper understanding of how painful or traumatic events in our lives affect the way we view the world, others, and ourselves. These views, sometimes known as core beliefs, affect our feelings and behavior in a cyclical triangle pattern. Taking stock might include events that happened to us in addition to acts that we participated in or behaviors we engaged in.

The cognitive triangle shows that our thoughts, behaviors, and feelings are all connected. Consider the following example:

You notice a man following you, walking quickly. You have the thought "I am in danger." You start to feel anxious. Your anxiety leads you to have the thought "I need to run," and you're prepared to start running.

But suppose you knew this man was chasing after you because you dropped your wallet a few blocks back. Your thought changes to "strangers are kind." You feel happy and grateful, and you decide to thank the man instead of run away.

From this example you can see how quickly our reactions can change once we change the way we think about a situation. Likewise, our thoughts can change when we aren't feeling heightened or upset.

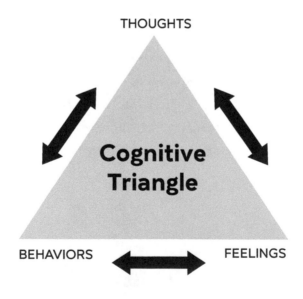

The wonderful part about the cognitive triangle is you can intercept it at any point if you find yourself in a negative cycle. Sometimes it's easiest to change our behavior, whereas other times we need to change the way we appraise a situation.

By examining our key developmental traumas, formative memories, and core beliefs more closely, we can learn to interrupt this vicious cycle and have a greater sense of control over our lives. It may seem counterintuitive, but it is only through the acceptance of the painful truths of our past that we can pave the way to a happier present and future.

Developing a Clear, Realistic View of the Past

When Angela was in high school, her mother used to throw lots of parties where she drank excessively. Angela watched her mother pour glass after glass of wine and make loud and inappropriate comments to guests. When Angela confronted her mother for saying something offensive to one of Angela's friends, her mother denied her drinking and accused Angela of "hearing things." She called her daughter crazy, and teased her for "not having fun." But now, as an adult, Angela has a hard time remembering details from when she was in high school and second-guesses some of her memories of the time.

When we have a clear, realistic view of childhood, we understand that we are the only ones with rights to our feelings, memories, and interpretations of events. No one else. This means we can rewrite our own narratives, and that is a crucial act of self-love. These narratives affect our beliefs about the world, our experiences, and ourselves.

Because of shame, fear, or a lack of self-awareness, alcoholic parents may deny that certain events occurred. This is called *gaslighting*. When our parents continually twist our reality like this, we learn not to trust our feelings, opinions, or intuitions. We might blame ourselves for others' actions or mistrust others without reason.

To unlearn the lies we were told, we must go back in time and reexamine our painful memories and relationships with a more critical eye. We can learn to explore these experiences with kindness and self-compassion, without self-blame or judgment. In addition to the work you'll do in this chapter, this process might involve speaking with trusted family members, looking through old journals and photo albums, attending a 12-step group, or speaking to a licensed professional.

Remember there is no one-size-fits-all approach; everyone recovers at their own speed. Learning to own your reality can be difficult, but it is not impossible. As an adult, you have the power to rewrite your story. You can start to show your inner child that it wasn't their fault, and that you can help them heal.

Coping with Complex Trauma

Growing up, Dani wasn't allowed to have friends or boyfriends or engage in extracurricular school activities. Her father strictly monitored, managed, and criticized how she spent her time. He claimed he did these things because he cared about her and wanted to keep her safe, but she grew up feeling suffocated and as though she were living in a fishbowl. As an adult, Dani has developed several health problems. She has a difficult time relaxing and having fun and is fearful of going on dates. Dani tells her therapist that she frequently feels like a small child in front of authority figures, and she shuts down instead of expressing herself. She also sees several doctors for frequent headaches and joint pain, but after exams, scans, and blood tests, none can ever find a medical root cause for her problems.

Complex trauma is characterized by a series of repeated traumatic events that have a cumulative effect on a child's social, emotional, or even physical development. It differs from other types of trauma in that the effect intensifies over time; it is not a singular, pinpointed traumatic event.

Complex trauma can be insidious and difficult to recognize. We might have grown up thinking that the behavior we experienced in our alcoholic households was normal, and that can lead us to tolerate similar mistreatment from partners, friends, and bosses. In cases such as Jane's, the body stores trauma physically. This leads to aches and pains or chronic illness that a doctor may not be able to explain. Complex trauma can also inhibit our ability to connect with other people, since we may fear or be unable to recognize healthy intimacy.

Identifying Complex Trauma

This exercise will help raise awareness about possible root causes for your current negative thoughts or behaviors.

Check off any of the past experiences that resonate with you. If you think of additional behaviors, write them in the provided space. (Remember, the term "parent" applies to any family member or caregiver involved in your upbringing.)

☐ My parent(s) lied to me on numerous occasions.

☐ My parents often put me in the middle of their arguments.

☐ My parent(s) blamed me for something they did.

☐ I was physically harmed by my parent(s).

☐ I was not allowed to have friends, romantic partners, or engage in other childhood activities.

☐ My parent(s) left me alone on numerous occasions at an age when I was too young to be without supervision.

☐ I recall worrying about my parent(s) from a young age.

☐ I frequently felt like my family was not "normal" growing up.

....

....

....

Journaling: Memory

The following exercise might bring up heavy emotions, as it is designed to heal the pain caused from a particular memory. Plan to have a self-care activity, quiet relaxation time, a favorite comfort food, or a phone call with a loved one afterwards, if needed.

Choose a memory from your childhood and, in the space, write it down in as much detail as you can remember. What were you doing and where were you? What did your parent do or say? Do you remember how the feeling felt in your body (pit in your stomach, tightness in your chest)?

Now, take a few moments to travel back in time to that memory, as though you are an adult visitor from the present watching the interaction unfold. What would you say to yourself as a child? How could you make that child feel safe, knowing what you know now as an adult? What does the child version of you need to feel comforted?

Finally, face your parent. As the caretaking adult you are, what would you say to your parent? What might they have said back to you?

You May Feel . . .

The next section focuses on how these past events have manifested themselves in your thoughts, feelings, and behaviors today. The excerpts and exercises might bring up anger, sadness, shame, or anxiety. Please know these reactions are completely normal, especially if you're taking an in-depth look at these parts of your life for the first time. A comprehensive list of these manifestations is difficult to provide because we react and internalize events vastly differently from one another. For the purposes of this book, the most common traits of adult children of alcoholics are covered.

A Lack of Healthy Boundaries

Although Tom's father held down a job, he blacked out three days a week. Sometimes, while drunk, Tom's father would yell at him and his mother for incomplete chores or for no reason at all. Tom saw that his mother never confronted his father about his drinking or the verbal abuse; in fact, Tom was often left to comfort his mother. He would join his mother the next morning in pretending that nothing had happened. As an adult, Tom has a hard time speaking up when responsibilities pile up at work. He also gets down on himself for staying with partners who take him for granted or play mind games.

We rely on our parents to model healthy relationships with others and with us. When they disrespect us, tell us our feelings don't matter, or can't communicate appropriately, they fail to teach us that boundaries are important and that our needs are valid. We cannot enact healthy boundaries if we've never learned them. As a result, we might learn to take responsibility for others and forget to focus on caring for ourselves.

This sense of responsibility and unstable relationship dynamics can manifest in people-pleasing behavior (for example: putting others' needs above your own), overexertion in the workplace, suppressing feelings, or tolerating mistreatment from others.

Missing Boundaries

This exercise will help raise awareness about areas to focus on going forward in your relationships.

Here are some examples of difficulty with boundaries. Check the ones that resonate with you.

☐ I have a hard time saying no.

☐ I worry people will be angry at me if I let them down.

☐ I take on too much of other people's work.

☐ I feel like I'm always caught up in someone else's drama.

☐ It's hard for me to speak up when I'm uncomfortable.

☐ I often overshare intimate details with people I don't know well.

☐ I put up with mistreatment from romantic partners, work colleagues, and/or friends.

Role-Playing to Set Boundaries

Role-playing is an integral part of rehearsing and internalizing new behavior so it comes more naturally to you when you really need it. This exercise will help you practice setting boundaries. It's best done when your counterpart can push back and challenge your boundaries in a realistic way. If a friend or therapist is accessible to you, you can role-play with them. Alternatively, you can practice on your own by saying them to yourself in the mirror

Check off any examples that you would like to incorporate into your daily vocabulary. Then imagine a specific situation where you could apply one or more of these phrases, such as while grocery shopping, at work, or with a romantic partner.

☐ "No, thank you."

☐ "Please don't talk to me like that."

☐ "I can't take on additional responsibility right now, but I'll let you know when I'm available."

☐ "I'd like to think about it before I agree."

☐ "Let's change the subject."

☐ "That doesn't sit well with me."

☐ "I'm not going to tolerate this anymore."

Self-Worth, Self-Esteem, and Confidence in Flux

Antoin grew up taking care of his alcoholic mother who never sought treatment for her bipolar disorder. He often turned down invitations to hang out with friends, chances to travel, and even job opportunities for fear that his mother would relapse. Although his mother is now sober and stable, Antoin struggles to create a fulfilling life for himself. He won't ask for a raise because he doesn't believe he deserves one, even though people less senior are getting promoted. Dating is also difficult, as he has trouble discerning when someone is taking advantage of him, believing he's lucky to be getting any attention from women at all. Because he's placed so much of his identity on being a helper, he has trouble thinking for himself and won't speak up or let himself acknowledge his own needs.

Self-esteem and confidence can be stunted in adult children of alcoholics for several different reasons. At times, parents actively erode a child's sense of self through abuse or neglect. But self-esteem can also take a hit from the well-meaning helicopter parents who try to control every aspect of a child's life. Similarly, as in Antoin's case, a child who is always worried about their parent as opposed to themselves learns to seek validation from others instead of from within. This often leads to excessive approval-seeking and trouble accepting constructive criticism or disagreement.

What Are My Issues with Self-Esteem and Self-Confidence?

In this quiz, you'll identify key issues with self-esteem and self-confidence and set the stage for further reflection in the next exercise. Place a check by each statement that resonates with you. If there were one or more that you didn't check off, keep them in mind for the reflection questions below.

☐ My mood and self-image are not determined by what other people think of me.

☐ I am decisive; I don't usually waffle when making choices.

☐ It's easy for me to voice my opinion or disagreement with someone.

☐ I am comfortable with who I am.

☐ I am compassionate with myself when I make a mistake.

☐ I enjoy my own company.

☐ Overall, I believe in my abilities.

☐ What I do matters.

Reflection Questions

This exercise will set you on the path to changing the negative script in your head.

If your self-confidence and self-esteem issues suddenly disappeared, how do you think your life would be different?

_____

_____

_____

_____

What did you want to do when you were younger that you didn't do because of your own harsh self-assessments?

_____

_____

_____

_____

How might you feel and talk to yourself to change these patterns? Write down some affirming statements to remind yourself what you're proud of.

_____

_____

_____

_____

Disconnect from Emotions and Feelings

When she was a young child, Kaitlyn used to plead with her father to stop drinking and smoking cigarettes. She was worried about his health. As a response, her father would switch the focus to Kaitlyn, telling her to stop eating junk food or staying up late because "that's not good for you either." And so, Kaitlyn grew up second-guessing herself. Now she has a hard time when her therapist asks her how she's feeling, because she never learned to trust her own feelings. She's discovering how much resentment she harbors for people who take advantage of her because she never sticks up for herself.

Alcoholics and parents who engage in other dysfunctional behaviors become experts at denial to back up their poor behavior. It's often easier for them to twist words, invalidate other people, or deny there's a problem than to face that problem. As adult children, consequently, we've learned that our feelings won't be validated or recognized. This is so painful that, over time, we gradually and unconsciously decide to stop having feelings altogether.

In a way, we shut down these feelings to protect ourselves from the pain of feeling unheard again or from the guilt of feeling like we made our parent uncomfortable. For you as an adult, the good news is that you can start to distinguish between what you are and are not responsible for, and that will help you get back in touch with yourself and with your feelings.

Difficulties with Emotional Expression

This quiz will help you identify if, or under what circumstances, you have trouble with emotional expression. Circle True or False for each statement.

1. Based on feedback from others, it often seems like my emotional responses are not appropriate for situations. **True / False**

2. I can easily recognize when I am angry. **True / False**

3. It's hard for me to answer the question "How are you feeling?" **True / False**

4. I believe it's better to keep feelings to yourself. **True / False**

5. It's more important to tell people how I feel than to avoid a conflict. **True / False**

Answer Key:

1. T = 1; F = 0
2. T = 0; F = 1
3. T = 1; F = 0
4. T = 1; F = 0
5. T = 0; F = 1

If you received three or more points, you likely have a difficult time with emotional identification or expression. Do not worry if this is the case. This book was designed to walk you through identifying, sitting with, and healthily expressing your full range of emotions. You'll learn that emotions are not experiences to be feared, but rather information to tell you something is wrong or an opportunity to learn about yourself.

Journaling: Your Feelings

What are the benefits to experiencing a full range of feelings? What helpful purpose might some painful feelings, like anxiety or anger, serve in your life, specifically?

....

....

....

....

Feelings of Guilt and Shame

When Dana got off the bus from school, she usually found her father passed out on the couch. She always went over to check if he was breathing. Her friends asked if they could come over, but she always made up an excuse. She didn't want them to see what she came home to, since she'd noticed their families didn't seem to have the same dynamic. Dana used to voice her concerns to her mother, but her mother never addressed them with her father or took Dana seriously. As an adult, Dana can't shake the sense that something is "wrong" with her, even though she knows she has no proof and can't quite put her finger on what she senses is "off" about herself. She worries about saying the wrong thing in social situations and ruminates when she returns home about what she might have said that was "wrong." She often assumes she is to blame for wrongdoings at work or in her friend group and finds herself compulsively saying "sorry."

Before we dive deeper into how our alcoholic home may have contributed to feelings of guilt and shame, it is first crucial to distinguish between these two emotions.

Guilt can be a healthy, internal response when we have made a mistake, done something that doesn't align with our values, or hurt someone's feelings. The automatic thought associated with guilt is typically some variation of "I did something bad."

Shame is an emotion that surfaces when there is a part of ourselves we feel disconnected from. It can happen when we imagine being ostracized or outcast from a group or if we are embarrassed about a part of our personality, body, or lifestyle. The automatic thoughts associated with shame might be "part of me is bad" or "I am bad."

Our parents may have unknowingly contributed to us experiencing these feelings when they weren't at all appropriate for the situation. For instance, we may have felt guilty or responsible for our parents if they blamed their drinking on us.

Similarly, as we explored in part 1, there is a silent creed in many alcoholic homes that we sweep the dysfunction under the rug and don't speak it into existence. This kind of invalidation can be very confusing for a child. When our parents do something to make us upset, disgusted, or angry and those emotions are not mirrored or accepted by our parents, we begin to wonder if we are the problem instead. This can lead us to misinterpret our feelings as wrong, bad, stupid, or irrelevant, leading to feelings of shame for having any feelings at all.

Remember that a certain level of guilt and shame is natural and healthy. If you cause someone harm or do something you aren't proud of, it makes sense that guilt would follow and that you would want to make things right. Similarly, everyone feels ashamed from time to time. It is important to offer yourself compassion to ease yourself through these moments.

Throughout your recovery, you will unlearn the unhelpful, inappropriate, and unnecessary guilt and shame that you grew so accustomed to in childhood. You'll learn to distinguish these feelings from healthy guilt and shame and to respond to yourself with kindness instead of judgment for experiencing a normal human emotion.

In the next two exercises, you'll practice distinguishing between guilt and shame. This is an important skill because we can easily mistake one for the other and unknowingly put ourselves through a lot of unnecessary pain in the process. Plus, when we can differentiate guilt from shame, we're also able to acknowledge when we are taking responsibility for something that isn't our fault.

Guilt or Shame?

Draw a line matching the thought with the feeling.

1. I did something I shouldn't have.

2. If I say how I feel, everyone will be disgusted.   **Guilt**

3. I feel bad about the way I talked to that person.

4. There's something wrong with me.

5. I need to keep this to myself.   **Shame**

6. This is my fault.

7. If they knew the real me, they wouldn't like me.

8. I caused this problem.

Answer Key:

1. Guilt
2. Shame
3. Guilt
4. Shame
5. Shame
6. Guilt
7. Shame
8. Guilt

Responding with Compassion to Guilt and Shame

Write about a time when feeling guilty or ashamed was a healthy or reasonable response.

_____

_____

_____

Write about a time when you felt guilty for something you didn't do or something you had no control over.

_____

_____

_____

_____

Think about a time when you were worried you would be ostracized from a group. Was this because of something with your family? Your culture? Your identity?

_____

_____

_____

Brainstorm some ideas for self-care to use the next time you feel guilty or ashamed.

....

....

....

....

Addictive Behavior

Aidan's parents got divorced when he was in kindergarten. For as long as he can remember, his mother couldn't tolerate being alone. She dated countless men, and as Aidan grew older, he realized how much his mother would change depending on the relationship she was in. Much like an alcoholic or substance abuser, Aidan's mother was inconsistent, unreliable, and chaotic. She often forgot to pack his lunches, attend his sports games, or pick him up from school because of her preoccupation with a relationship or a breakup. Because Aidan grew up learning to associate relationships with chaos, he hasn't opened himself up to any romantic partners and feels safer alone.

Kyle's mom has chronic back pain. After a particularly painful post-operative recovery, her doctor prescribed her opioids. She became addicted and hid this addiction from Kyle for several months. Although his mom has been in and out of recovery twice and has been doing well, Kyle feels on edge every time she mentions she's in pain or comes back from a doctor's appointment. He has nightmares about her relapsing and often visits or checks in with her by phone five or six times a day to make sure she's not abusing any medications. To cope with his anxiety, Kyle has started drinking more than usual, at times to the point where he can't remember how much he drinks.

Substance addiction is just one of many possible addictions that our family members may have struggled with. Some of our parents may have battled with gambling, gaming, compulsive spending, or codependency. Addiction can be passed down from parents to children; in fact, at least half of a person's vulnerability to drug addiction can be linked to genetics. In addition, the presence and amount of a certain type of dopamine receptors, which play an integral role in how we experience pleasure and happiness, has been associated with a greater risk of becoming addicted to alcohol, heroin, and cocaine.

However, this doesn't mean we can rule out the importance of environmental factors. As adult children, we may have picked up unhealthy habits from parents that later turned into addictions or overcompensated by developing other issues with moderation or impulse control. This might include excessive shopping, difficulty budgeting money, drinking more than we would like to in a sitting, or even speaking out of turn or interrupting frequently.

In addition, growing up with an alcoholic parent who is using, moving in and out of recovery, or displaying other unhealthy behaviors once recovered can be unsettling, confusing, and frustrating to say the least. It was hard for us as children to learn how to appropriately regulate our emotions and self-soothe because we didn't have a model for what that looked like. More likely, we watched our parents drink or drug their own uncomfortable feelings away or cope with their life stressors in other unhealthy and addictive ways, as noted in the vignettes on page 28.

As we explored previously, guilt and shame are rampant in alcoholic homes, and because these feelings can be so confusing and painful without quick fixes, many of us learned to self-medicate in unhelpful ways. Perhaps our self-regulation was not exactly like our parents' forms of self-soothing, but the goal remained the same: to numb or avoid the pain in some way.

This insight may be the first step in getting treatment for your addiction. Here are some exercises designed to screen for substance abuse disorders and other compulsive disorders. If you score highly on one or both sections, I strongly recommend reaching out to a licensed substance abuse counselor or other therapist, as you may not find this book sufficient to meet those treatment needs. (You'll find some suggestions for locating a therapist in the Resources on page 138.)

Self-Screen

Place a check by the statements that have applied to you during the past six months.

☐ I have trouble controlling my drinking and/or substance use.

☐ Friends and family tell me I need to cut back on my drinking or substance use.

☐ I feel guilty about my substance use or drinking.

☐ My substance use or drinking has gotten in the way of my work or family obligations.

☐ I often don't remember what I do after I've used my substance or after I've been drinking.

If you placed a check on at least two of these, you may have a substance abuse problem.

Impulse Control Screening

Place a check by the statements that have applied to you during the past six months.

☐ When I need something, I usually purchase multiples of that item.

☐ I can never have just one, whether it's a cookie or a glass of wine.

☐ I can't leave a store empty-handed.

☐ There is something very soothing about spending a lot of money.

☐ I know I have too many things in my home, but I can't bring myself to throw them away.

☐ It's hard for me to say no to food, even if my body tells me I'm not hungry.

If you checked one or more of these items, and they are interfering with your day-to-day activities or relationships, you may want to seek help for compulsive behavior.

Identifying Off-Limits Feelings

What feelings seem off-limits to you? In other words, which feelings might you not allow yourself to fully feel? Examples might include stress, contentment, anxiety, pride, anger, sadness, or disappointment.

_____

_____

_____

For the off-limit feelings you listed, what behaviors do you use to distract, cope, or avoid those feelings? Next to each coping skill, write a little note about whether that behavior is more helpful or harmful to you.

_____

_____

_____

Depression and Anxiety

In Anna's home, she grew up feeling like she wasn't valued or loved. Both of her parents are alcoholics, and, although she feels she has a decent relationship with them, she's been chronically worried about their health and behavior for as long as she can remember. As Anna progressed from adolescence into adulthood, she started getting more and more fearful about leaving the house and often felt very sad, unmotivated, and tired. Because she's afraid of getting close to too many people, she often feels isolated, which also contributes to her down mood.

Depression can feel like relentless sadness or irritability. It might include loss of interest in your favorite activities, drifting away from friends and family, and feelings of hopelessness and helplessness. Mundane tasks might feel completely overwhelming. You may notice yourself comparing your life to others', filtering out all that you're grateful for and instead focusing on the dreariness and negativity of your life and the world around you.

These behaviors and feelings are usually accompanied by low energy or restlessness, noticeable changes in sleep or appetite, trouble concentrating, and suicidal thoughts. However, it's important to note that depression is nuanced and different for everyone. Some folks might cycle between highs and lows, with the lows more pronounced and profound, whereas others experience a mild or moderate depression as their baseline, making it difficult to discern when they are feeling "better" or "worse." Depression can make you feel like you're not engaging in a meaningful life, or you might feel as if you're simply existing at times.

Anxiety is broad term that can refer to a generalized anxiety disorder (feelings of worry, dread, or nervousness accompanied by ruminating thoughts), phobias (specific fear of objects or scenarios), or obsessive-compulsive disorder (characterized by intrusive unwanted thoughts and compulsive behaviors to stop those thoughts). Anxiety can also make it very difficult for an individual to carry out their important daily tasks and engage meaningfully in relationships.

Many adult children also struggle with panic attacks, intrusive memories, nightmares, overthinking, chronic worrying, and social anxiety. These are likely linked to the post-traumatic stress of growing up in an emotionally unsafe environment. But just as with depression, anxiety can manifest itself differently in every person. We all respond to trauma in vastly different ways. The key is to learn how it has affected you personally and how you can be uniquely kind to yourself as you recover.

There are a couple of possible explanations for why depression and anxiety are common in adult children of alcoholics. Many alcoholics self-medicate in response to underlying mood or anxiety disorders, which can have a genetic component. It's possible these genetic proclivities can be passed down to us. Our home environment and relationship with our parents also can interact with these genetic factors and make depression and anxiety more likely. For instance, as a result of growing up in her home, Anna may have developed a core belief that she is not worthy or that people are untrustworthy. These core beliefs could then make her depressed or anxious.

If we think about the family as a system, each part plays a particular role in maintaining the function of the system. When one part starts to malfunction, another has to step in and work overtime; other parts might get burned-out or angry and shut down altogether. It is therefore possible that each sibling will develop different ways of coping with the various traumas that can occur in an alcoholic home. Much like depression and anxiety, coping skills are both learned and genetic. One sibling may prefer to take care of everything and ensure the family "stays running," whereas another might detach entirely to protect themselves.

It can be easy to harbor resentment, frustration, and general confusion over why your siblings chose to cope in a different way from you. Sometimes, the harm simply may be too deep and complex to heal. But it is understandable for us to want to mend these broken relationships. Traveling through the path of recovery without a companion can be lonely, and sometimes, if both parties are willing to be vulnerable, we can find great comfort in sharing our feelings and experiences with someone who grew up in the same home as us.

Control Issues and Difficulty Handling Change

Diedre's home was very chaotic while she was growing up. Her parents had a hard time communicating and keeping schedules straight. Often, they didn't follow through on promises. Diedre now has a hard time with relationships because when someone doesn't meet her expectations or lets her down, she gets very angry and finds it hard not to be judgmental. She's also extraordinarily self-critical, especially when running late or when her ideas do not go as planned.

In an alcoholic home, there are many different relationships parents can have with control. This may manifest as:

- **Overcontrol:** rigid organization, inflexible expectations, strict dieting or exercise regimens, using anger to enforce rules, manipulation, difficulty with vulnerability
- **Lack of control:** carelessness, disorganization, forgetfulness, binge eating, trouble sticking to a routine, poor boundaries, oversharing
- **A mixture of both:** hoarding, an eating disorder that involves binging and purging, drinking or using a substance in excess to try to control or suppress emotions

Remember that not all relationships with control are dysfunctional. We need control to regulate ourselves and move about the world in a way that benefits ourselves and others. Sometimes we learn important lessons from our family and internalize that we don't want to repeat their behaviors. For instance, someone who grows up with a parent who hoards might become incredibly self-disciplined.

A crucial turning point in recovery is the realization that we actually have control over ourselves and the way we choose to interact with and react to our environment. This is the essence of the serenity prayer:

Grant me the serenity to accept the things I cannot change;
The courage to change the things I can;
And the wisdom to know the difference.

Exploring Control

What is my relationship with control? This exercise will help raise awareness about how control issues can manifest in different ways. Circle or highlight the statements that are true for you. For any that aren't true, make notes on those you aspire to make true for you throughout recovery.

General Sense of Control

I handle change well.

When things don't go as planned, I generally don't have too much trouble adjusting.

I feel in charge and confident with the life decisions I make.

Control over Emotions

I feel okay to share with others how I'm feeling.

Emotions are an important, acceptable part of life.

I am able to regulate myself when I get upset.

Control over Others

Other people's feelings, thoughts, and behaviors are not my responsibility.

I am not the expert in someone else's life.

Control over Spending

I exercise restraint with purchases.

I spend within my means.

Control over Body

I intuitively listen to my hunger cues and desire for movement and exercise.

I nourish my body appropriately.

Journaling: Control

How has control helped you in your life?

_____

_____

_____

In what ways have you tried to have too much control?

_____

_____

_____

In what areas do you think you could exert more control?

_____

_____

_____

Recurring or Toxic Relationship Patterns

From as early as infancy, our tiny minds start to form a general idea of what relationships are meant to look like. If we're lucky, we have healthy attachments with family members and go off into the world thinking it's a safe place.

Unfortunately, growing up in an alcoholic home, this sense of trust and safety can be fractured by abuse, neglect, manipulation, or parentification. As a result, we may not fully believe we're capable or deserving of a nurturing, reliable attachment. We might think arguing, fighting, and lying are the norms and continue to seek out partners who exhibit these behaviors; after all, it is all we know.

As adult children of alcoholics, we might get frustrated by our relationships because it seems like each one continually echoes the dynamics, toxic communication patterns, or abusive behaviors from previous relationship patterns. It's easy to get discouraged and give up on intimacy altogether.

You may find it helpful to view your relationships as mirrors. Each one will reflect back to you the issues, dynamics, or beliefs about yourself that you still need to heal. Gradually, as you start to change, your relationship dynamic and the people you allow into your life will change for the better as well.

My Relationship Patterns

Put a check by the statements that resonate with you.

☐ I ignore or don't know how to look for red flags in relationships.

☐ I seem to encounter the same problem, relationship after relationship.

☐ I tend to take all of the blame for the problems in my relationships.

☐ I end up getting into casual hookups or emotionally unavailable relationships only; I desperately want more but I'm scared.

☐ It's hard for me to ask for what I need in my relationship.

☐ The negative parts of my relationship resemble what I disliked most about my relationship with my parents.

☐ Sometimes, I would rather swallow my feelings than express them to my partner.

☐ I am caught up or have been caught up in enabling situations with partners in the past.

Being a Friend to Yourself

Pick the quality that resonated with you the most. Now, imagine a friend or loved one is coming to you with the same problem. What would you say to them?

....

....

....

....

Chapter Wrap-Up

I hope this chapter has been helpful and has shed light on some of the core challenges you've faced as an adult child of an alcoholic. You may like to make note of any exercises, sections, or insights you found particularly helpful. You can take them a step further by journaling in more depth about the impact they had on you or by sharing with a therapist.

When we reflect, accept, and offer ourselves compassion for the difficult experiences we've had, it allows us to slowly start shedding the shame that has built up for so long. As we continue to undo and unlearn messages and lessons that no longer serve us, we will see how we can enrich our lives in the present. That's what you'll learn about in the next section.

PART TWO

Living in the Present

Now that we've learned to take stock of how certain patterns of behaviors from childhood may have manifested themselves in our lives, we can shift our focus to healing. The chapter ahead will focus on specific skills you can use to help cope with the various ways alcoholism has affected you and help you live a more fulfilling life.

CHAPTER THREE

Let Yourself Grieve

"Maybe instead of slamming the door on pain, I need to throw open the door wide and say, Come in. Sit down with me. And don't leave until you have taught me what I need to know."

—GLENNON DOYLE, *LOVE WARRIOR*

This chapter will help you process the many losses that are inherent in growing up in an alcoholic home. You'll notice that not all of the vignettes, explanations, or definitions include death of a family member. This is because grief can extend far beyond physical loss of human life. Some people, for example, grieve over the loss of their own childhood. If you did not lose a parent or other family member, you will still be able to relate to this section.

Why We Grieve

Yuki is an only child. Both of her parents were alcoholics, but her father passed away when she was 12 years old due to complications from his alcoholism. Her mother stopped drinking but struggled on and off with depression and an eating disorder. Yuki didn't make many close friends and didn't have time to engage in extracurricular or social activities because she was always taking care of her mother. She grew to view downtime, hobbies, and socializing as frivolous, unnecessary activities and became suspicious and judgmental of those with free time. When she finally went away to college, she quickly realized that many of her friends had had different, more secure homes than hers, with two parents who were attentive. She noticed her friends had had the support to develop into healthy young adults, whereas Yuki very much still felt like a child. She started working with a college counselor on grieving the loss of her childhood so it wouldn't prevent her from enjoying her college experience. Yuki is now learning about playfulness and the value of relaxing and having fun, and she's exploring her own interests.

Grief is not limited to death. What we grieve for can take many forms. Often, we must grieve for the loss of normalcy, the unmet expectations of our parents or other loved ones, a failed relationship, broken trust, the loss of fantasies we developed to keep ourselves safe, or a life without mental or physical illness.

If we do not appropriately process grief, it may show up as depression, anxiety, difficulty concentrating, or a fear of intimacy.

Grief Is Essential to Healing

Grief is crucial to the healing process because it reorients us to reality. The sadness, anger, confusion, and longing are important to process so we can appreciate all the opportunities ahead of us. Grief allows us to fully embrace, understand, and have feelings about what we have lost or have never had.

Although acknowledging the absence or loss of something can be painful at first, it's a necessary step in acceptance. Once we're able to acknowledge it, we can then focus on how we would like to honor or cope with that loss or absence in a healthy way.

Grief also allows us self-acceptance. We can recognize that we did the best we could with the knowledge, resources, and support that we had at the time. Through self-acceptance, we are more able to forgive others. When we forgive, we let go of feelings that may be toxic to us and prevent us from moving on.

The following is a series of exercises that will help you identify, process, and let go of your sources of grief. You'll find it most effective to move through them in order from start to finish. The exercises might bring up painful feelings, so it is completely normal to take a little break and come back to them another day. In fact, that's an excellent form of self-care!

If you find you don't have enough writing space in this workbook to complete any one of these exercises, you may like to keep a journal nearby and continue writing in it.

Taking Stock

This exercise will help you identify and grieve things you may not have known you had lost.

In the first column of the following exercise, write down a comprehensive list of everything you lost, had to give up, or didn't experience as a result of growing up in an alcoholic or dysfunctional home. Your responses might be concrete, like the loss of a person's life, or more abstract, like happy memories or a sense of security.

Identifying Emotions

Grief brings up a lot of unresolved emotion. Through identifying and allowing emotions, we stop the cycle of self-judgment.

Next to each loss from the previous exercise, write down one or two emotions that come up when you think about that loss. Here are some examples of feeling words, but feel free to come up with your own: angry, sad, frustrated, despair, lonely, furious, left out, ashamed, embarrassed, uneasy, unsafe.

LOSS	EMOTIONS

How Has Grief Affected Me?

This exercise helps us look at grief through a series of lenses. Revisit the Taking Stock exercise and choose the loss that affects you most as an adult today. Then explore it further by responding to the following questions.

What negative qualities did I develop as a result of this loss and that I might like to change? Write a list.

What positive qualities did I develop as a result of this loss? Write a list.

How did this loss make me more resilient? Were there ways I changed for the better as a result?

Offering Self-Compassion

In this exercise we'll rehearse positive, compassionate self-talk. Doing this regularly helps the habit become more accessible in times of need.

Take the list of negative qualities about yourself that you wrote down in the previous exercise. Perhaps because of your loss you're hypercritical of others, fearful of new situations, or extremely hard on yourself. For each quality, close your eyes, and repeat the following phrases to yourself:

I forgive myself for developing [negative quality]. This was a normal response to an abnormal situation. I am learning to love myself and all of my qualities.

Writing a Letter to Your Parent

Letter writing can be an emotional release that allows you to let go of resentment, anger, or other feelings that might be holding you back.

Write a letter to your alcoholic parent, expressing in unfiltered words how you feel about the things you experienced and what was taken from you.

If you are able, feel free to add a section about forgiveness. You might use the letter as an opportunity to move forward. However, this is not necessary. Some wounds are too deep, and we may not be ready to forgive them yet. In this case, a letter explaining your feelings is enough.

Writing a Letter to Yourself

There is no greater gift you can give to yourself than the time and space to connect to the you within.

Imagine you're looking at yourself as a child sitting across from you. Generate as much love and compassion as you can and write your inner child a letter. You might choose to focus on how what happened to them was not their fault, or offer them a peek into what adulthood has to offer and all they will accomplish. Offer comfort.

Sharing Is Caring

Sharing our feelings with someone we care about is one of the most effective ways to eradicate shame about our experiences. Here are some ways to introduce the work you are doing in this workbook to other people:

"I've been doing a lot of work on myself lately; I really trust you, and I'd like to share some of it with you."

"I want to tell you some things about my (childhood, parents, or family) but I'm a little nervous. I'd prefer if you just listened for a little, and then we can talk afterward."

"I've been struggling with (shame, anger, sadness) a lot lately, and I think I know why. I'd like to tell you some things I've been through that have made me who I am."

Please know this exercise is completely optional. Many memories are painful enough for us to remember, let alone share with someone else. The most important person to share your healing with is yourself, so please don't feel pressure to do this particular exercise if you're not ready. You may also want to practice with a therapist first.

Self-Care Ideas

Because recovery can be a long process, it's important to contribute to your self-care toolkit as often as possible.

Look back at the Taking Stock exercise (page 43). Take note of the experiences you feel you were robbed of as a child and the things you may have missed out on. Choose two and brainstorm some ideas for how you might give those things to yourself now, as an adult. For instance, if you have trouble relaxing, write down some creative ways to work breaks into your workweek. If you feel unsafe in your own home, brainstorm some sensory ideas to facilitate a calming environment.

1. ....

....

....

2. ....

....

....

When you're done, pick one or two activities you can implement right away.

Chapter Wrap-Up

I hope this chapter has helped provide some insight into your relationship with your grief and how to move forward. Please keep in mind that emotions around grief tend to ebb and flow with seasons, anniversaries, and other big life events. You can return to the exercises as needed for some extra self-care! These exercises will be a nice complement to our next chapter, which is about connecting more deeply with our emotions and self-awareness.

CHAPTER FOUR

Connect with Your Emotions and Cultivate Self-Awareness

"I now see how owning our story and loving ourselves through that process is the bravest thing that we will ever do."

—BRENÉ BROWN, *THE GIFTS OF IMPERFECTION*

Now that we've had a taste of making peace with our grief, we can move toward accepting and embracing our emotional experience. As adult children of alcoholics, this may be a new phenomenon. Feelings may have been taboo in our homes, swept under the rug, ignored, or invalidated. Here, we retake control over our experiences. We learn we cannot only tolerate but learn to love and appreciate all of our feelings and what they are here to tell us.

Exploring Your Emotions

As a child, when Tanner cried, his parents usually did not respond to him. He was often left to comfort himself, and as he grew a bit older, he came to understand and expect that no one was responding to his emotional expression. As an adult, he has a difficult time verbalizing when he is upset, taken advantage of, or angry. Tanner's unable to find the vocabulary or at times even identify his feelings.

Connecting with our emotions is a crucial part of healing because it allows us to validate ourselves and make sense of our experiences. Emotions tell us when things are dangerous, pleasurable, questionable, fun, or scary; they are our internal compass.

In childhood, if our feelings are not validated, we might grow up thinking emotions are problematic. At times, our parents were unable to respond appropriately to our needs, so we may have shut down our feelings to avoid punishment or to try to be perfect children.

Gender roles may also have played a part; women may be told not to be dramatic or hysterical, whereas men may have been sent the message that emotions are a sign of weakness. Members of the LGBTQIA+ community, any historically racially or religiously oppressed group, and those with disabilities may also relate to feeling invalidated not only by their families at home, but by society at large. If there were ever parts of our identity that did not feel safe or welcome to emerge, it is important to offer extra loving-kindness and compassion to those parts of ourselves and to seek support in the community. One of the wonderful parts about recovery is that our families no longer have to define, restrict, or shame our identities; we can make space for chosen families, communities, and support systems that share our values.

Connect with Who You Are

Jodi's moms were both high-powered executives who worked around the clock together at their own firm. One of Jodi's mothers was an alcoholic and frequently ran into problems at work, so her wife often had to cover for her and work overtime. Jodi grew up watching her parents devote all of their time to work and none to personal interests, socialization, or relaxation. As a result, Jodi grew up thinking it was normal to abandon self-interests in service of work. She feels empty after work hours. On the weekends, Jodi feels the need to fill her time with activities she considers productive, but experiences decision paralysis when she tries to find hobbies.

A sense of self means we feel grounded in who we are. We're able to reconcile our internal experiences (opinions, thoughts, emotions, personal goals) with our external experiences (acting in accordance with our values, how we show up in relationships, other behaviors). We have a stable and consistent idea about who we are, what we like and dislike, and how we show up in the world. We respect our sense of self when we express our feelings and surround ourselves with people who love us. In addition, having a sense of self means we are aware of our shortcomings and areas we may want to work on.

Adult children of alcoholics do not always have fully developed identities. As children, we often retreated into fantasies, which kept us from developing the resources needed to understand and respond to reality. This could be because our parents intentionally or unintentionally distorted that reality for us or were not good guiding posts to let us get to know our feelings and interests on a deep level. Issues pertaining to culture, religion, race, class, disability, and other factors affecting family dynamics also go into the development of our identity—or, perhaps, a rejection of our identity.

Developing an identity is important because it helps us move through the world and interactions with others with confidence. When our inner and outer worlds are aligned, we can know true peace. The following exercises are designed to help you get more in touch with who you are at your core.

Identifying Emotions

As we've discussed in previous sections, as adult children it's difficult for us to identify our emotions. This exercise will help you see the nuances in your core emotion and give you a greater emotional vocabulary.

Here are some examples of core emotions. Circle or highlight any you experience often.

Anger: bitterness, annoyance, frustration, rage, grumpiness

Fear: nervousness, anxiety, tenseness, worry, uneasiness, panic

Happiness: joy, glee, pleasure, excitement, satisfaction, amusement

Jealousy: cautiousness, mistrust, possessiveness, wariness

Love: adoration, liking, kindness, passion, infatuation, longing

Sadness: grief, disappointment, hurt, rejection, feeling crushed, suffering, loneliness

How Do You Experience Emotions?

This exercise will take emotion identification a step further.

Of the emotions you highlighted above, consider the following:

- In what situations do they tend to occur?
- What changes happen in your body?
- How comfortable are you expressing this emotion?

....

....

....

....

....

....

Exploring Your Psychosocial Identity

This exercise will help you reclaim your personal narrative and remind you that only you have the power to define who you truly are.

The word *psychosocial* refers to the psychological and social factors that contribute to our identity development. Use the categories to write a brief statement about who you are.

- Age
- Gender identity and pronouns
- Ethnicity
- Race
- Sexual orientation
- Citizenship status
- Birth order
- Place where you were born
- Where you grew up
- Mental or physical conditions
- Occupation
- Education level
- Marital status or relationship status
- Parental status
- Religion, if applicable

....

....

....

Giving Yourself Permission to Develop Interests

As an adult, you can give yourself and your inner child the permission to play, explore, and have fun. This exercise explores how.

Write a list of areas you'd like to explore more about yourself. Some examples include:

- Political beliefs
- Hobbies
- Exercise or physical recreation
- Musical preferences

Say out loud to yourself: "I give myself permission to have wants, needs, likes, and dislikes. I understand this is a lifelong learning process and that I will change a lot. I'm excited to begin that process now." When we speak affirmations, intentions, and wishes, we allow our voices to be heard, which can be a powerful phenomenon. It allows us to say to ourselves that our needs can take up space.

List of Positive Qualities (How would a friend describe me?)

This exercise helps us get out of our own head for a minute and lets us see ourselves the way someone else might see us.

Think of someone you know who cares deeply for you. Close your eyes and picture yourself asking them, "How would you describe me?" Take a moment to let it sink in, and then journal about what your loved one said.

Role-Playing

This exercise takes emotional expression a step further.

Refer back to the exercise How Do You Experience Emotions? (page 51). Note the areas where you have a hard time expressing your feelings. Then write out an imagined dialogue with a loved one on the lines provided. As you write, think about these questions: How do you want them to react to you? How do you fear that they will react to you? What is the worst thing that can happen if you express your emotions to that loved one?

You may also like to practice expressing your emotions aloud by role-playing with a trusted friend, loved one, or therapist.

Identifying Values

While growing up, we may not have been taught that it was okay to live by our own values. This exercise will help you get in touch with what really matters to you.

A big part of owning who we are is living by our values. Here are some common examples of values. Circle or highlight the ones that mean the most to you.

Family

Spirituality

Personal growth

Relaxation and leisure

Physical and mental health

Career development

Romantic relationships

Friendships

Community and activism

Do you have any values that you feel aren't represented by this list?

....

....

....

Choose one value and reflect on it.

....

....

....

....

Living by Values

Now, reflect more deeply on the values you've circled. Ask yourself the following questions:

- On a scale from 1 to 10, how actively am I living out this value?
- What are actionable behaviors I can do to increase my lower scores?

Use the space to list and rate the values you'd like to work on and write the actions you can take to better realize these values. I've added some suggestions:

Value: Family (living by it at a 6/10)

Actions: Call my grandparents two times a month and visit once a month.

Value: Health (living by it at a 5/10)

Actions: Keep up with my medical and dental appointments.

....

....

....

....

....

....

....

Chapter Wrap-Up

I hope that after learning more about what it means to connect with yourself, your identity, and your values, you've begun the journey to more deeply develop your own wants and needs. As I mentioned earlier, learning about and owning your reality is a lifelong process that will change over time just as we change over time.

Having this connection with ourselves is a crucial foundation for the next step of our healing process, which will focus on finally putting down the burdens of guilt and shame that we've likely carried from our childhoods.

CHAPTER FIVE

Heal Guilt and Shame

"Shame closes the heart to self-compassion."

—FRANCIS WELLER, *THE WILD EDGE OF SORROW*

In this chapter, we'll take a deeper look at the roles guilt and shame played in our childhood and how they may be manifesting in present-day relationships. We'll look at why shame is so common in alcoholic families. You'll learn how to spot your shame triggers and how to heal yourself from within. You'll also learn some tips for talking to others about topics that may seem shameful to you, because connection is an incredibly important part of healing.

What Are Guilt and Shame?

Kieran's parents drank so much that they had a hard time getting him ready for school and making sure he had clean clothes, fresh lunches, and school supplies. At school, he always had the feeling other kids were staring at him, making fun of him, or purposely keeping their distance. He has grown up with a lot of shame, particularly about his appearance and his possessions.

Tara's mother got pregnant with Tara when she was young and always tells Tara how much easier her life would have been if Tara hadn't been born. She also blames Tara for her drinking problem, claiming that all of the long nights, stress, and everything she gave up to be a mother drives her to drink. Tara feels excessively guilty as an adult, even though at times she does not understand why.

Although they are commonly seen as interchangeable, guilt and shame are distinct feelings resulting from two very different thought processes. When someone feels guilty, they worry they have done something bad. If you feel excessive guilt, you might believe you're burdensome to others. You may apologize frequently, avoid taking up space, or worry about making others uncomfortable.

On the other hand, shame is the feeling that something is wrong with you as a person. This might have to do with a quality about you, such as your body type, sexual orientation, class, race, or other personality type. It may revolve around a person or family secret that, if revealed, you fear would ostracize you socially.

We learn to internalize guilt and shame both directly and indirectly. In the story above, Tara's mother told her she was an inconvenience. But sometimes children can feel guilty for their parents' alcohol use. They may grow up unknowingly taking on the mental burden that they could've stopped the use, if only they had been better, more obedient, more lovable, more vocal.

Adult children internalize shame from their childhood homes when expression of feelings was not welcome in a household. Some describe this as a feeling of always having to walk on eggshells, feeling self-conscious about bringing friends over to meet their family, or a subtle understanding that their family is different from their friends' families. When we grow up with such a foundation, it can be difficult to internalize that it is safe for our feelings to be acknowledged in present day.

Guilt, in appropriate doses at appropriate times, can be a healthy emotion. We want a child to feel bad if they hurt another child; it's normal to feel remorseful if we lashed out at our partner in the heat of the moment. Often, guilt helps us take responsibility for our own behavior and take the first step to make amends with people. What we want to look out for is when we take on guilt that is not ours, such as taking responsibility for others' feelings or behaviors, living in "what if" and "if only," and apologizing for things that weren't our fault.

Shame has a bit of a different history and function. At its very basic level, shame exists to alert us that we're going to be rejected by or shunned from our community or social group if we tell our true story and show our true colors. It wants us to hide who we are and to keep us from sharing how we feel. This feeling, like all feelings, has a well-meaning purpose designed to protect us and ensure our survival.

But now, as adults, we may have discovered the feeling has stayed beyond its welcome. We may want desperately to learn how to love ourselves, even the parts of ourselves that were banished or hidden for so long. The good news is we now have the power of discretion. We can choose to share our story with a selection of compassionate, caring, nonjudgmental people of our own choosing. We do not have to continue suffering alone.

It's Family-Related and It's Personal

Adult children of alcoholics share a unique bond when it comes to their experiences with guilt and shame. Dysfunctional behaviors such as drinking, substance use or abuse, and neglect are often hidden from the rest of the world. As children, we quickly learn to keep such happenings within our home and at times, must put on an act in the "real world."

As a result, many children grow up feeling embarrassed by or unsure of their own feelings. This can lead to shame about certain feelings, like resentment, sadness, or fear. Think of it as a double serving of shame: As children, we felt shame about what went on in our homes which later led to developing more shame about our own feelings.

In order to move through guilt and shame, we must first gain a greater understanding of the inner workings of each emotion. The following exercises will progress from identifying and understanding to accepting and, finally, to healing. They'll help you distinguish if you're holding onto your own guilt or someone else's, connect with the parts of you that feel shame, and walk you through ways to feel less alone in your struggles.

Identifying Shame

Here are some examples of how shame might show up in your life. Circle or highlight all that apply to you and feel free to add more examples.

Worrying excessively about not being "enough" in some capacity

Fearing that if you're vulnerable about some aspect of your life or past, others will reject or judge you

Leaving certain parts of your life out of conversation when getting to know someone

Experiencing physical symptoms of flushed cheeks, difficulty keeping eye contact, or a feeling of shutting down emotionally

Having frequent automatic negative thoughts such as "I am bad," "I am defective," or "There's something wrong with me"

_____

_____

_____

_____

Identifying Guilt

Here are some examples of how guilt might show up in your life. Circle or highlight all that apply to you and feel free to add more examples.

I feel responsible for other people's behaviors, feelings, and reactions.

I give myself a very hard time when I make a mistake.

I feel uneasy when I have to tell someone no, knowing they'll likely be disappointed.

Sometimes it's hard to tell where my family members' needs end and mine begin.

If something bad happens as a result of my boundary, I believe it is my fault.

When something bad happens, I can't help but wonder if I could have done more to prevent it.

_____

_____

_____

_____

Meditation for Allowing Emotions to Surface in the Body

Meditations are wonderful ways to connect with our breath, slow our heart rate, feel more present, and give ourselves permission to feel things we may have repressed. At the very least, meditation serves the purpose of carving out time in your day just for you.

The purpose of meditation is to learn to respond to changes in your body with compassion and curiosity, as opposed to judgment and fear. Our body holds a lot of tension that often does not make it into our conscious mind. By attuning to these changes inside, we can figure out how to respond to and soothe them.

You can follow the steps, or you may want to record your voice reading this meditation and then play it back for yourself. Another option is to ask a trusted friend, family member, or professional to guide you through it. (You can also find body scan meditations on the mobile app Insight Timer, or find one with audio on YouTube.)

To begin, choose a space where you can sit comfortably with your feet on the floor. Turn off any electronics or other distractions if possible. Note that you can choose to close your eyes or soften your gaze slightly downward on something that isn't moving.

1. *Before closing your eyes, take a look around the room and notice everywhere there is a boundary. This includes walls, ceilings, and floors. Notice how it feels to be contained safely in this space. These boundaries provide structure for you.*

2. *Next, bring your attention to any exits. This might include a door, windows, or other passageways. Notice how it feels to know you can move around at free will.*

3. *Close your eyes. Feel your feet on the ground. Take a deep breath in and hold it for 4 seconds, exhale for 4, hold for 4, and then repeat. Stay for a moment, breathing at your own pace. When you feel comfortable, start to bring your attention to anything in your body that might be calling out for your attention. It might be a feeling of tension, tightness, slight pain, or a vague discomfort that you can't quite label.*

4. *Picture an orb of warm light passing over this part of your body, smoothing out the tension. When you breathe in, the light expands. When you exhale, it gets a little smaller. Imagine this orb giving your body energy and peace at the same time.*

5. *Notice how your relationship to the discomfort changes as you continue to breathe through each part of your body that needs attention. If a mantra should come naturally into your mind—something such as "It's okay" or "You're safe"—feel free to stay and repeat it for as long as you need.*

Journaling: Shame

Imagine a life without shame. How would your day-to-day world look and feel different? Are there things you would or wouldn't do? What would you let go of?

Journaling: Guilt

Reflect back on the examples you circled in the Identifying Guilt exercise (page 62). Then categorize these examples and any others you can think of into one of the two columns in the table. (I've filled in an example to get you started.)

THINGS I AM RESPONSIBLE FOR	THINGS I AM NOT RESPONSIBLE FOR
My behavior	*Other people's behavior*

What Behaviors Are Enabling My Shame and Guilt?

Take a look at the list and circle or highlight any that resonate with you. Feel free to add additional examples.

Apologizing profusely without reason

Saying yes when there's already too much on your plate

Putting out other people's fires before your own

Telling people what they want to hear, even if it's not speaking your truth

Remaining in an uncomfortable situation for fear of hurting others' feelings

Shutting down emotionally and being unsure of why

Loving-Kindness Meditation/Visualization

Similar to the Meditation for Allowing Emotions to Surface in the Body (page 63), you can practice this meditation on your own or under the guidance of a trusted friend, family member, or professional. You can also find loving-kindness meditations on the mobile app Insight Timer, or find one with audio on YouTube. The purpose of the meditation is to open your heart with compassion and kindness.

1. *Start sitting in an upright position with your feet on the floor and your back preferably against the back of a chair. Relax your arms in your lap. Close your eyes. Take a few deep breaths. Imagine a young child, perhaps someone from your family or friend group, is walking toward you. Notice their appearance, how they seem to be feeling, if they are talking to you, anything about them. Now, imagine yourself saying to them, "May you be happy; may you be healthy; may you be at peace." Repeat it as many times as you'd like before letting them walk away.*

2. *Next, imagine a stranger approaching you. The stranger can be someone of any gender and age; perhaps it is someone you see often in your local coffee shop or grocery store. Imagine them walking toward you and see them in as much vivid detail as possible. Repeat the same phrases to them when you are ready: "May you be happy; may you be healthy; may you be at peace." Imagine yourself feeling the authenticity of your words.*

3. *Now imagine a beautiful mirror of any kind and of your preferred style. Visualize yourself stepping in front of the mirror. Notice how you look. Do you seem tired? Have you been crying? How are you feeling? Is it written on your face or concealed in some way? Take yourself in, however you are feeling. Then repeat the kind words you've been saying to others to yourself: "May I be happy; may I be healthy; may I be at peace." When you are ready, open your eyes.*

Letting Go

This is an opportunity to get creative in a metaphorical way with your guilt and shame. Through a variety of different activities, we can come up with a way to help you let go of some of your burdens. Here are some examples.

- Use a sticky note or scrap of paper to write down every memory, relationship, unhelpful behavior, or negative thought pattern you would like to let go of. If you have a fireplace or a place to safely make a fire outside, start a fire and slowly place each piece of paper into the fire, honoring your intention to let it go.

- If you live near the ocean or another body of water, collect stones, shells, or other items from nature. Let each item represent something you'd like to stop carrying with you. Feel the release of letting go as you throw it into the water.
- Make a list of the things you'd like to let go of. Practice affirmations in the mirror, repeating the following: "[What you want to give up] no longer serves me. I will work to leave this behind me. Instead, I will practice [another behavior, thought pattern, or goal]."

Chapter Wrap-Up

As a gentle reminder, please do not consider these efforts a failure if reminders of your shame and guilt continue after these exercises. It can take a while before new learned behavioral and thought patterns fully sink in. You can revisit this section whenever you need and feel free to complete any of the exercises again. The goal is progress, not perfection. We are human. Painful memories can sometimes persist longer than we'd like them to, but that doesn't mean you have done anything incorrectly.

This chapter and these exercises pave the perfect path toward our next chapter on boundaries, which are highly linked to guilt and shame. I hope you can use these exercises as building blocks for our next level of resilience!

CHAPTER SIX

Construct Healthy Boundaries

"Boundary systems are invisible and symbolic 'force fields'
that have three purposes:
(1) to keep people from coming into our space and abusing us,
(2) to keep us from going into the space of others and abusing them, and
(3) to give each of us a way to embody our sense of 'who we are.'"

—PIA MELLODY, ANDREA WELLS MILLER, AND J. KEITH MILLER,
FACING CODEPENDENCE

Now that we've gained an understanding of guilt and shame, connecting with ourselves more deeply, and the importance of grief in this work, we can learn to start detaching from others with love—in other words, the art of boundaries.

Boundaries are both acts of self-love and important methods of communication. They set the stage for a healthy way of coexisting with the people we love and can reduce a lot of suffering and tension. In this section, we'll explore exactly what that looks like while also engaging in some specific exercises to facilitate boundaries.

What Are Healthy Boundaries?

Carl is a 40-year-old single man who grew up with an alcoholic mother, with whom he no longer has a relationship. Carl watched his father, Matthew, enable his mother for years, never confronting her about her drinking or neglectful behaviors. Through these experiences, Carl learned that helplessness is a way to get what he wants. Often, he doesn't take care of himself. Although he has a decent job, he spends outside of his means. Matthew still makes Carl's doctor's appointments and pays for most of his rent and other overhead costs. Matthew is starting to resent Carl but doesn't know how to stop his financial support because it's been going on for so many years. Plus, Carl goes into a rage whenever his father threatens to stop financing his life, leading Matthew to feel very guilty.

Healthy boundaries consist of the following qualities:

- Both parties feel safe to express their needs, within reasonable limits of those needs.
- Both parties respect each other's needs to the best of their ability.
- Neither party gaslights or downplays the other's needs.
- If contact is unwanted, that wish is respected.
- A person understands they can walk away from a situation that makes them uncomfortable.
- Both parties do not overreach or take it upon themselves to solve others' problems without that person asking for help.
- There is no triangulation, which means no involving a third party in your conflict resolution.
- Secrets are kept confidential.

Setting boundaries is an act of self-love, but it's also an act of love for the other person. Healthy boundaries follow a clear set of guidelines that allow you to engage with another person safely and effectively. These are the foundations of a successful, caring, and respectful relationship.

It is kind to help others, but when we pour and pour from our own cup into someone else's, our cup eventually runs dry. Then we can't hydrate ourselves! Boundaries are here to make sure this doesn't happen. They allow us to preserve our emotional energy to focus on our own resilience and self-care.

Boundary-setting is not about changing your family member's personality or their behavior; it is more an act of self-care for you. However, boundaries often do elicit positive behavioral responses from others when done compassionately and consistently.

Give Yourself Permission

Throughout these passages and exercises, remember that you have a right to set these boundaries. No one can control your behavior except for you, and for many people this may mean taking back that control for the first time in a long time, or ever. Being assertive doesn't come naturally to everyone and that is okay; in fact, in the therapy world, assertiveness training is a very common reason for people to seek help.

Check in with yourself and acknowledge any discomfort that comes up when you think about being assertive, and give yourself permission now to experiment with it. It might be uncomfortable in the short term, but in the long term you will gain strength, confidence, and more peace.

Remember that the only person's behavior you can control is your own: You can set boundaries, but it's up to the other person to respect them. While boundaries eventually might cause a positive shift in behavior from your family member, remember that this is not the primary goal and does not determine your worth or success in setting the boundary. The real value in setting limits is to show yourself love and emotional safety. Above all, you must do what feels safe and healthy for you, even if that means making the boundaries less and less flexible over time if they continue to be disrespected.

Unfortunately, people may react poorly to your taking care of yourself at first, especially if you have engaged in people-pleasing habits or have not previously stuck up for yourself. Your family member might accuse you of being rude, manipulative, or simply "having changed a lot." Remember, change does not mean you're doing it wrong! If you continue to set the boundary in spite of the discomfort it causes, consider that a success for you. Make sure to take care of yourself and try not to internalize hurtful comments about your new, positive habits. Defend your right to a healthy life.

In addition, keep in mind that these exercises might bring up times when you, instead of your loved one, have been the one to cross boundaries. This is understandable, as loose boundaries tend to run in both directions. Keep an open mind and remember the benefits from these exercises will be twofold.

Identifying Areas Where I'd Like to Set Boundaries

Write an exhaustive list of people and/or behaviors that cross your boundaries. Here are two examples to get you started:

My brother asks me for money every week.

A date that I rejected continued to contact me after I told him I wasn't interested.

_____

_____

_____

_____

_____

_____

_____

_____

_____

_____

Identifying Areas Where I Cross Others' Boundaries

Using the first exercise as inspiration, are there any areas where you might need to recognize and respect other peoples' boundaries? This might be tougher, but think of the work you did in chapter 5 and areas where you take responsibility for others. Here are two examples for you:

I push the food that I make onto others even though they say no.

I reach out to my direct reports when I know they're sick or on vacation.

_____

_____

_____

_____

Assertiveness Training

Marsha M. Linehan's *DBT© Skills Training Handouts and Worksheets* provides a very useful exercise that helps with assertiveness. The acronym for the exercise is DEAR.

Describe: *Stick to the facts of the situation and tell the other person exactly what you are concerned about.*

"You continue to show up drunk to family gatherings and it makes me uncomfortable."

Express: *Tell them your feelings and opinions, and don't assume they already know how you feel. Use "I" statements to avoid defensiveness.*

"It makes me worried for your health and concerned for the grandkids to see you like that."

Assert: *Ask for what you want or say no clearly. Others cannot read your mind, so be direct.*

"I love spending time with you when you're sober. Please do not show up if you're drunk."

Reinforce: *Reward the person ahead of time by explaining the positives of complying with your boundary. Also be clear about the negatives if they do not listen.*

"It would make me and the grandkids happy to spend time with you sober. But if you can't agree, I won't let you in."

Write down some assertive statements of your own for each section of DEAR that apply to a boundary you'd like to set and then practice them to yourself in the mirror. If you'd like to take it a step further and have people accessible, you can also practice this exercise in a role-play with a therapist or loved one you trust.

Adding More Helpful Language

Now that we've reviewed a healthy process for setting a boundary, it's time to focus on the content. Sometimes, short statements without a lot of explanation behind them can pack a bigger punch than long, drawn-out explanations. Try incorporating these into your vocabulary by reading them aloud to yourself or writing them down, or imagine using them in scenarios where you find your boundaries crossed:

"This is really important to me, and I'm not going to change my mind."
"I'm not going to tolerate it anymore."
"This behavior is hurting me."
"I'm going to [boundary] if you don't [stop the problem behavior]."
"I'm not purposely hurting you; I'm doing what's best for me."

Coping with Manipulation

Sometimes, our loved ones will push back. They might know what our weaknesses are, how to appeal to our emotions, or how to get us to feel guilty. Thankfully, Linehan also provides tips for these curveballs in her manual.

- Practice keeping your focus on your goals; maintain your position, and don't get distracted. Thinking of yourself as a "broken record" can help with this: Keep saying no or expressing your opinion over and over. Imagine you're a politician who needs to stay on message during a debate.
- Ignore personal attacks or threats. Do not respond to them. It is an attempt to get you off track. Keep making your point.
- Appear confident. Use a confident tone of voice and stand physically tall.
- Practice not whispering, not interrupting yourself, or looking downward. Avoid unclear phrases like "I don't know."
- Assert your boundary. If it feels like a safe or accessible option, you can push back on the other person for ideas by asking a question like "What do you think we should do?" This allows them to have some involvement in the decision-making.

Think about a boundary you'd like to set. Write down some assertive, direct, and confident language you might use to express it to someone.

_____

_____

_____

What do you anticipate their response might be?

_____

_____

_____

What is the worst-case scenario?

_____

_____

_____

What is the best-case scenario?

_____

_____

_____

What do you think is most likely to happen as a result of setting these boundaries? How can you problem-solve for that situation, if necessary?

_____

_____

_____

Whom can you call for support or encouragement if you're struggling with self-doubt afterwards? What kind or compassionate words might they say to you?

_____

_____

_____

Building Relationships with Family

This exercise will help you take a critical look at your family and your individual relationships with them. Use the space to journal about the following:

- Whom do you consider your primary family?
- How strong is your relationship, on a scale from 1 to 10?
- What values do you share? What values do you have different views on?
- What might be the biggest roadblocks to improving your relationship?
- What are some immediate behavioral steps you can take today to start repairing your relationship while still respecting the boundaries you want to set? For example, "I will limit my time with them to once-a-month visits."
- Would the person be open to a frank conversation about improving the relationship?

_____

_____

_____

_____

_____

_____

_____

_____

....

....

....

....

Affirmations for When Things Get Difficult

Unfortunately, you may receive backlash when you start to set boundaries. It can be uncomfortable for our loved ones to see us change, for a variety of reasons: they're envious, they don't like the "new us," it's forcing them to look at themselves, or it's inconvenient for them.

This is the point where many people drop off and stop developing their boundaries. But not you! You will pick an affirmation from this list and place it where you can see it on a regular basis, like on your fridge, your phone background, or a sticky note in your car.

Boundaries are an act of love.

This situation is unsustainable, and I want to change.

Their feelings about my boundaries are not my responsibility.

Sometimes taking care of myself feels difficult and that's okay.

Write down some affirmations of your own:

....

....

....

....

A Record of Success

In spite of the pushback you might get, it is incredibly important to log your successes as your own form of reinforcement. Often, we need to pat ourselves on our own backs because we don't have someone to do it for us. So, if you can remember, capture the boundaries you set here. They can be simple ("I said no to extra pie at dessert") or very difficult ("I told grandpa he can't come to Thanksgiving unless he's sober.")

Remember, the *response* of the person is *not* your goal. The goal is to *set the boundary for yourself*! If grandpa shows up drunk to Thanksgiving or if your mother-in-law gives you that extra piece of pie anyway, it doesn't mean you failed. Your act of setting the boundary is what we need to celebrate!

Chapter Wrap-Up

I hope this chapter has helped you explore more deeply some of the ways you've struggled with boundaries and, more importantly, some ways you can make them stronger. I encourage you to remember this is a practice, not an end goal. It may take some time before it becomes more second nature to you.

Boundaries are one of the building blocks of self-confidence and self-esteem, which are the topics of the next chapter, so I hope you find that the self-awareness you gained here continues to grow!

CHAPTER SEVEN

Build Confidence and Self-Esteem

Self-esteem is not about reaching a point where you have found perfection within yourself; it is seeing yourself for who you really are, flaws and all, and choosing to love yourself anyway.

In this chapter, we'll learn about why adult children of alcoholics struggle with self-esteem and the unique challenges we face. The exercises in this chapter will examine and build crucial components of self-esteem, including self-compassion, self-acceptance, and self-care. It is my hope that by the end of this chapter, you have a road map to the areas of self-esteem in which you would like to continue growing.

Finding Self-Confidence and Self-Esteem

Carissa is a single woman in her 20s. She recently landed her dream job in her favorite city but finds herself timid at work. She's afraid to ask questions or seem incompetent. Her boss praises her consistently, but she focuses on the minor criticisms, often leading her to feel like an impostor. Carissa has a hard time trusting herself and is in therapy to work on her relationship with her parents. Her father tells her that he's proud of her but often in the context of backhanded compliments to highlight the class differences between them, such as "Since when are you a rich, fancy girl?" Carissa knows she has worked hard to get to where she is, and yet she still has trouble trusting herself.

As we explored in previous chapters, our reality was twisted when we were children. We may have been told we were good one moment, only to be berated or neglected when our parent was using or drinking. If we bounced around households growing up or didn't have a stable caregiver, we may have learned not to have trust in the world or in other people.

Our parents may have been very critical of us to the point where our strengths, creativity, and positive attributes went completely unnoticed. This can lead us to question our integrity, our abilities, our opinions, and even our interests. Because our caretakers are the ones who are supposed to know best, we do not wonder if they are at fault. Instead, we internalize the criticism and relentlessly judge ourselves.

Similarly, when we become old enough to realize that our parents are not acting in healthy ways but still don't understand why, it can be easy to turn some of our anger inward towards ourselves. This can lead to thoughts such as "There must be something wrong with me if this keeps happening in my home."

These environments are breeding grounds for self-doubt, insecurities, and trouble trusting ourselves. As a result, we might end up in situations that replicate our family dynamics, which further reinforce the beliefs we already had about ourselves and the world, continuing a vicious cycle that's hard to get out of without some awareness.

Embrace the Discomfort

Building self-confidence and self-esteem will not only help you have a healthier relationship with yourself, but also will allow you to be more present and compassionate with others. Learning and strengthening these habits comes from changing your behavior first, which may feel strange, uncomfortable, or even false at first. This is perfectly normal.

Think about this: Sometimes in yoga, cycling, or meditation classes, the instructor will ask you to smile slightly, unclench your jaw, and relax your shoulders. This immediately sends a message to your brain that you're more relaxed and open. The same happens when we practice confident behaviors; over time, the more we act a certain way or engage in certain habits, the more our bodies and our minds become familiar with them and incorporate them into day-to-day life.

In these exercises, you'll more clearly identify your concerns about self-esteem and self-confidence and learn some skills for building them.

Identifying Areas to Work On

Read the list of common struggles with confidence and self-esteem and rate them from 1 to 10, with 1 meaning you don't struggle at all and 10 meaning you struggle often.

- I have a hard time voicing my opinions.
- I judge myself very harshly, more than I do my loved ones.
- I have a lot of thoughts like "I will be happy once I . . . (lose weight, get a new job, find a partner, etc.)."
- I have very frequent negative thoughts about myself.
- I find myself in situations where friends or partners treat me poorly.
- I'm not proud of many things that I've done.
- I don't believe I'm worthy of my accomplishments or accolades.

Motivating Yourself to Work on Self-Esteem

Answer the following questions:

- How is my low self-esteem and/or low self-confidence affecting me on a day-to-day basis? Aim for two to five specific examples.
- How would my life be better if I had more self-love and self-acceptance? Aim for two or three specific examples.

_____

_____

_____

_____

_____

_____

_____

_____

_____

_____

_____

_____

_____

_____

_____

_____

Learn to Identify Cognitive Distortions

A _cognitive distortion_ is a fancy word for a thinking error or an automatic negative thought that is unproven or unhelpful to you. The following are some red flags that you might be experiencing cognitive distortions:

- **Binary thinking** such as _always, never, all the time, everybody._
- **Catastrophizing** or immediately jumping to the worst-case scenario.
- **Mental filter** or when one ignores all positive/neutral aspects of a situation and only focuses on the negative.
- **Mind reading** or believing you know what someone is thinking or going to do.
- **Personalization** or blaming yourself for an event over which you had no control.

Next to each example, write down which category the vignette or sentence falls under.

1. Kami's roommate usually says hello to her after she gets home from work, but today she went right into her room quickly and shut her door. Kami said to herself, "Great, she's mad at me for something I did, I just know it."

   Cognitive distortion: _____

2. Parker received a text from a man he went on two dates with expressing he was not interested in pursuing a relationship. Parker immediately thought, "No one will ever be interested in me."

   Cognitive distortion: _____

3. Sandra found out her partner was cheating on her. She keeps telling herself that she drove him to cheat because she worked too much and "didn't try to look pretty enough."

   Cognitive distortion: _____

4. Mateo's boss put a one-on-one meeting on his calendar. Mateo's first thought is "I'm going to get fired."

   Cognitive distortion: _____

5. Kat sent a picture of herself in a dress to her group chat of five friends. Four of her friends sent positive emojis and words of encouragement to buy the dress, and one friend said she didn't like the color on her. Even though she felt good in it, Kat didn't buy the dress, convinced it looked terrible because of her friend's comment.

   Cognitive distortion: _____

6. Vivek has to give a presentation in class but can't stop worrying that he's going to completely freeze and sweat through his clothes and that the entire class will start laughing at him.

   Cognitive distortion: _____

Answer Key:

1. mind reading or personalization
2. binary thinking
3. personalization
4. catastrophizing
5. mental filter
6. catastrophizing

Noting Your Own Cognitive Distortions

Reflect briefly on your past week or so. Think about your personal relationships (work, family, friendships). Which cognitive distortions resonate the most with you? Write them down. (The first example is provided as reference.)

Binary thinking: Today, my boss kept the door shut the entire day and was in a foul mood. He really is a lousy person through and through. He doesn't have any redeeming qualities.

....

....

....

....

Personalization

....

....

....

....

Mental filter

....

....

....

....

Mind reading

_____

_____

_____

_____

Catastrophizing

_____

_____

_____

_____

Arguing with Your Cognitive Distortions

It's important to respond to cognitive distortions with a thought that is balanced, rational, and either neutral or, ideally, positive. This is how we can rewire our thinking.

Here are some examples of ways to counter your negative thoughts. Check off the ones that you think would work best for you.

☐ **2:1 ratio:** For every negative possible scenario or aspect of a situation you notice, challenge yourself to also notice two positive things about the situation.

☐ **What would a friend say?** As simple as it sounds, talk to yourself like a friend would.

☐ **Defense attorney:** Challenge your black-and-white thoughts with examples of times your thought very clearly was not true.

☐ **Probability:** Think about or research the probability of your thought coming true, if applicable.

☐ **Worst/Best/Most Likely:** After going through a worst-case scenario in your mind, ask yourself about the best-case scenario; then let yourself settle on what is most likely to happen.

Putting Your Arguing into Action

Pick two or three examples that resonate the most with you from the previous exercise. Write them in the left column of the table that follows. In the middle column, note how that thought makes you feel (angry, sad, anxious). In the third column, pose an alternative, more balanced, rational thought to yourself. In the final column, note how that alternative thought changes how you feel. The first example is provided as reference.

You can also read over the chart and keep it in the back of your mind in case you come up with examples later on. You may want to recreate this chart in a journal to make monitoring your thoughts a daily practice.

COGNITIVE DISTORTION	FEELING	ALTERNATIVE THOUGHT	FEELING
"Every time I open myself up, I get hurt."	*Angry, sad*	*"There have been times I've opened up to friends and it's gone well. I will get hurt sometimes but that's part of life."*	*A little more relaxed, hopeful*

COGNITIVE DISTORTION	FEELING	ALTERNATIVE THOUGHT	FEELING

Positive Qualities

Very rarely in life is anything ever completely one way or the other. The stories we learn from our parents are usually only one-sided and do not paint a full picture.

Here is a list of positive qualities. Circle the ones that describe you. Please note it is not an extensive list, as we human beings are far more complex than can be captured in a list, but hopefully it's a starting point. Blank lines are included for you to write down other qualities that come to mind.

If this exercise is difficult, try imagining the person who loves you most in this world filling out the list for you. How would they describe you? This is the way you want to learn to talk to yourself.

☐ Generous

☐ Kind

☐ Compassionate

☐ Funny/has sense of humor

☐ Understanding

☐ Dedicated

- ☐ Honest
- ☐ Creative
- ☐ Reflective
- ☐ Helpful
- ☐ Has sense of fashion/style
- ☐ Athletic
- ☐ Committed to goals
- ☐ Gives good advice
- ☐ Hard worker
- ☐ Good listener

- ☐ Resilient/bounces back after challenging times
- ☐ Quick learner
- ☐ Focused
- ☐ Empathetic
- ☐ Role model for others
- ☐ Self-sufficient
- ☐ Organized
- ☐ Optimistic
- ☐ Rational
- ☐ Levelheaded

Affirmations

Part A: Use the traits you circled or wrote down in the previous exercise and write them down on something you can make visible in your home. It can be on your fridge, a sticky note on your mirror, your computer background, or anywhere you'd like to see these words of self-affirmation.

Take it a step further and journal about behavioral examples of these traits at the end of each day. For instance, "I am kind. Today, I saw the man in front of me struggling to pay for his coffee so I bought it for him." It's okay if some of your examples come from others acknowledging you, such as "My coworker thanked me for listening to her." But try not to rely too heavily on external validation. The point of this exercise is for *you* to feel good about *yourself*.

Part B: Perhaps in the previous exercise, you noticed while reading the list that there were many qualities you did not believe you possessed. It's possible this made you sad. The good news is that everything you want to become is already inside of you. Identifying what you want to work on is the first step toward achieving it!

Write down the traits you want to strengthen. Then, write yourself a quick story about what someone with that trait does on a daily basis. What kinds of thoughts might they have? What kinds of people might they hang out with? How do they handle disappointment or setbacks? How do they talk to themselves?

Chapter Wrap-Up

Remember that awareness is the first step to any form of change. I hope these vignettes and exercises will help you embrace the parts about yourself that you honor and love and that you have a blueprint for further strengthening your self-confidence and self-esteem. It will prepare you well for the next section, which is focused on self-love.

CHAPTER EIGHT

Love Yourself

"Practicing self-love means learning how to trust ourselves, to treat ourselves with respect, and to be kind and affectionate towards ourselves."

—BRENÉ BROWN, *THE GIFTS OF IMPERFECTION*

Learning to love ourselves is a crucial foundation for changing thought patterns, behaviors, and the ways in which we show up in relationships. When we're able to extend love and compassion to ourselves in times of need, it helps us offer that same kindness to others, which in turn enriches our lives.

The Importance of Self-Love and Self-Compassion

There are several key components to the art of self-compassion and self-love:

- Recognizing that you are suffering
- Refraining from judging your suffering
- Approaching your thoughts, behaviors, and experiences with a curiosity and an open mind
- Recognizing that growing, learning, and changing are all healthy and normal parts of human development
- Offering yourself forgiveness for making mistakes or for when you slip back into patterns of self-criticism
- Being patient with yourself
- Giving yourself permission to enjoy activities you love
- Accepting yourself for who you are

Keep in mind that self-compassion does not mean you stop owning accountability or taking responsibility for your behaviors. Rather, it enables you to take responsibility for all the parts of you, not just the critical and self-judgmental parts.

Self-love might vary from person to person, as each person takes care of themselves in different ways, but most self-love pathways involve the following milestones and practices:

- Learning to identify your inner voice or knowing what is right and wrong for you
- Allowing your inner voice to guide your decision-making process
- Taking care of your body. This might include a skin care routine, regular bubble baths or hot showers, stretching, or an exercise routine that helps you stay present.
- Sticking up for yourself when someone violates your boundaries or mistreats you in another way
- Choosing to surround yourself with a loving, caring, and validating support system. Keep in mind this support system need not be entirely like-minded with you. In fact, it can be healthy to expose yourself to different viewpoints to expand any narrowness in your opinions.
- Defending your self-love routine to the best of your ability. This means not letting competing responsibilities, like work or a relationship, consistently interfere with your ability to take care of yourself.

Self-compassion and self-love are essential to healing because they help us return to ourselves and re-center ourselves. As adult children of alcoholics, we may be accustomed to hiding or denying our feelings, enabling others' behavior, or blaming ourselves relentlessly for our struggles. Self-compassion and self-love invite us to dismantle this narrative and consider the possibility that we are human and sometimes must work to achieve and maintain our happiness.

How Self-Love Helps

In her book *Self-Compassion*, psychologist and researcher Kristin Neff writes about the benefits of self-love and being kind and forgiving with ourselves.

"Research shows that self-compassionate people tend to experience fewer negative emotions—such as fear, irritability, hostility, or distress —than those who lack self-compassion. These emotions still come up, but they aren't as frequent, long-lasting, or persistent. This is partly because self-compassionate people have been found to ruminate much less than those who lack self-compassion."

The work of building your self-love and self-compassion is critically important. The following exercises are designed to help you remove obstacles to self-compassion and self-love and learn more about what each might look like in practice in your daily life.

Journaling: What's Getting in Your Way?

This journaling exercise will focus specifically on developing self-compassion. When we're able to speak kindly and nonjudgmentally to ourselves, it sets us up well to practice this behavior with others, thereby strengthening our relationships.

Ask yourself these questions: What stops you from self-compassion? Is it the way you talk to yourself? Can you not forgive yourself for mistakes? Are you afraid of taking chances or going for your goals? Use the provided space to reflect upon this.

Show Yourself Love

There are many ways we can show ourselves love. We can nourish our bodies, feed our intellectual mind, or express an emotion we've been holding in. This exercise will help you get in touch with all the kind things you do for yourself.

Write down ways to show yourself physical or emotional love. After you write each down, categorize them by physical, emotional, or both. The first three are filled in as examples.

ACTIVITY	PHYSICAL LOVE	EMOTIONAL LOVE
Brushing my teeth	X	
Cooking my favorite meal	X	X
Allowing a good cry without judgment		X

"I Am Allowed to . . ."

As children, we often felt we didn't have permission to express our feelings, be ourselves, or act like the kids that we were. This exercise will work on undoing some of that hesitation.

Write down the things you get the most self-critical about. Then, practice repeating them with the phrase "I am allowed to . . ." in front of them, either to yourself, a loved one, or a therapist.

Examples:

I am allowed to get angry.

I am allowed to let others down.

I am allowed to say no.

....

....

....

....

....

....

....

....

....

Enjoying Your Own Company

Keep an activity log of things you do just for the sake of doing them for yourself. Feel free to make copies of this chart for future weeks. Doing this will give you a sense of how you could strengthen your pleasurable activities. Also, making a conscious effort to notice where and when you're enjoying yourself will lead you to focus more on joy than sorrow.

TIME OF DAY	MORNING	AFTERNOON	EVENING
SUNDAY			
MONDAY			

→

TIME OF DAY	MORNING	AFTERNOON	EVENING
TUESDAY			
WEDNESDAY			
THURSDAY			
FRIDAY			
SATURDAY			

Now add some goals, setting your own schedule. For example, you could list two self-love activities a day or one for each time of day.

....

....

Acknowledging Suffering

As adults, sometimes we forget that we know more than we did as children. This exercise will be an opportunity for you to re-parent yourself.

Write a list of times you've suffered throughout your life. Then, imagine you're talking to yourself at that age or writing yourself a letter from the point of view of an understanding, compassionate version of yourself.

....

....

....

....

....

....

Replacing Judgmental Self-Talk

Passing judgment is second nature to us as adult children. You might feel as though you have to work extra hard at being compassionate. The following chart will walk you through how to start changing your thought process.

Think for a moment about a situation in which you could have acted more self-compassionately. Perhaps more than one situation will readily come to mind. Journal about an alternate way you could have handled the situation or talked to yourself about the situation. The first is an example to help you get started.

SITUATION	SELF-TALK	BEHAVIOR	HOW I'D DO IT DIFFERENTLY TODAY
I spilled red sauce on my friend's carpet	*"I'm such an idiot. I can't do anything right."*	*Apologized profusely and continually throughout the night; verbally berated myself in front of everyone*	*I would express my deepest guilt and apologies and tell myself that guilt is a healthy emotion when a mistake is made. I would forgive myself.*

Affirmations

Affirmations rewire the way we think about others and ourselves. They may feel fake and unnatural at first, but practice makes progress. Taking the time to repeat them can make a huge difference. They can help us show up more in our personal relationships by being more present.

Circle the affirmations that resonate with you and write down any others that come to mind. Repeat these affirmations daily as needed to strengthen your relationship with yourself. This will allow for greater presence in your relationships with others as well.

I am learning to love myself.

I will practice patience with myself today.

I have positive qualities that I appreciate.

I will do at least one thing to take care of my body today.

I am deserving of love.

I do not have to engage with people who bring me down.

My behavior and responses are within my control.

(When applicable) I am suffering right now, so I will take it easy.

Make Time for Things You Love

How often do you do something just for you, because you enjoy it? In her book *You Are a Badass*, Jen Sincero makes an excellent point about making time for the things we love: "When you constantly deny yourself the people, food, things, and experiences that make you feel the most alive, that sends a pretty lousy message home."

Use the space to write down some of your favorite activities. There is no limit or right or wrong answer; simply reflect on what brings you joy and write it here. This will also allow you to reflect on the relationships in your life that bring you joy.

Now, set a small, reasonable goal that involves incorporating some of these activities into your life. You might say, "I will do X amount of these activities once a week, once a month, or when I feel sad."

Chapter Wrap-Up

Throughout this chapter, we've explored how to practice self-love and self-compassion. These skills are intricately woven into our relationships with other people. Being self-compassionate and kind to ourselves helps us set the stage for the way we want to be treated by others and also helps us give other people the same respect we give ourselves.

The next chapter will be dedicated to the wholesome, fulfilling, and healthy relationships that lie ahead for you. We'll look at how to build them, nurture them, and keep them strong.

PART THREE

Loving Your Future

Many of us may feel as though the chance for healthy romantic relationships, friendships, or family relationships has been robbed from us. Based on what we experienced growing up in an alcoholic home, it is common to feel hopeless and helpless when thinking about building a partnership with someone. Where do I begin? How would I know what to say? What if I don't recognize red flags?

These chapters will help you navigate those questions and more as we explore what it means to be in a healthy relationship.

CHAPTER NINE

Building and Navigating Healthy Relationships

"And I know for sure that in the final analysis of our lives—when the to-do lists are no more, when the frenzy is finished, when our email inboxes are empty—the only thing that will have any lasting value is whether we've loved others and whether they've loved us."

—OPRAH WINFREY, *WHAT I KNOW FOR SURE*

In this chapter, we'll look at the defining characteristics of healthy relationships and see how boundaries and red flags come into play. We'll learn how to distinguish a healthy relationship from a potentially unhealthy one. We'll also discuss the different dynamics that come up in friendships compared with those in romantic relationships.

Healthy Relationships

Jesse and Victoria have been dating for two years. Jesse grew up in an alcoholic home, and Victoria struggled with verbal and emotional abuse from her father during her early life before he left the family. Jesse and Victoria have arguments occasionally, but they understand this is part of any relationship and that it doesn't mean they have to go to extremes and break up. They also understand after several years of being together that Victoria needs a day or so to cool down after a fight before they can have a productive conversation. Similarly, Jesse detaches when stressed. She's aware of this issue and is actively working on it. Victoria has come to understand and accept it, and she's learned to ask for what she needs calmly. Neither partner takes it personally when the other wants alone time or time with their respective friends. They feel safe and able to express their needs, even if that means gently criticizing each other.

As we can see from this vignette, Jesse and Victoria's relationship is not perfect. They argue and disagree; both have their own "stuff" from childhood that they need to work on. The most important thing is that Jesse and Victoria talk to each other and try to understand each other. It will be hard to have empathy for your partner 100 percent of the time, especially if they do something hurtful. But in a healthy relationship, both parties work to understand each other for the purposes of strengthening their connection and commitment.

Here are some key components of a healthy intimate relationship:

- **Boundaries.** In a healthy romantic partnership, two people can coexist but also maintain a sense of their own independent needs and feelings. Partners ask each other permission before doing anything that could make the other partner uncomfortable. Boundaries are also not so rigid and inflexible that they can't change over time; they allow for adaptation as the comfort level grows.
- **Shared values.** Values are the principles that guide our behavior. For instance, if we value community, we may donate several times a year if we can or volunteer at a local organization. If we value our career, we might invest a lot of time and money in our education to get where we want to be. It's important to clarify your own values and your partner's values to see if you can accept any discrepancies.
- **Trust.** Partners prove to each other that they're reliable, consistent, and safe. Examples of this are showing up when you say you're going to show up, staying emotionally present during stressful times instead of detaching, and being honest.
- **Shared interests.** In the honeymoon phase, it might seem as if your only shared interest is each other, which can feel wonderful! But as the old adage goes, "Love does not consist in gazing at each other, but in looking together in the same direction." It's important to be fully present with the world and to have a hobby or an activity together to avoid getting lost in each other.
- **Commitment.** Healthy relationships won't necessarily stop just because life inevitably gets tough. Partners understand what they must do to stay devoted to each other. People in

healthy relationships understand "commit" is a verb—it's an action they must keep doing. They understand relationships don't survive purely on the feeling of love or infatuation.

- **Realism.** Seeing your partner's flaws is more indicative of love than idealization. We all have imperfections! When we idealize our partners, it can feel rosy and warm at first, but in the end, we're only harming ourselves by not acknowledging the existence of some real roadblocks we may need to work through in terms of communication, values, or lifestyle.
- **Emotional support.** Partners can lean on each other for advice, concrete help, or simply validation and support about their emotional experience, especially if difficult. Similarly, partners are cheerleaders for each other during exciting times in their lives, such as a promotion or other accomplishment.
- **Sacrifice and compromise.** There will be times when you or your partner will have to give up something you enjoy or love or spend time doing things you *don't* enjoy or love. A one-sided relationship often builds resentment.

Healthy friendships have similar qualities to intimate relationships and, ideally, share the same qualities, although friendships might have fewer formal check-ins about how the relationship is going. It's important to note that true friends will *not* do the following to one another:

- **Abuse one another's emotional bandwidth.** An unhealthy dynamic occurs when one friend continually uses the other friend as an outlet for his or her problems without being able to offer that same support to the friend.
- **Insult frequently.** Friends who bring each other down to make themselves feel better or to try to be funny in front of others simply because they are insecure are not friends.
- **Invalidate.** People who insinuate their problems are worse than yours or tell you that you don't have anything to be upset about do not have your best interests in mind.
- **Triangulate.** Friends who talk about you to other friends instead of directly to you about a problem do not have appropriate communication skills and do not know how to handle conflict.
- **Control.** If you feel like a friend is trying to mold you into who they think you should be (clothing, career, other lifestyle choices), be wary. True friends accept you for you—*all* parts of you.

Starting from Scratch

Building a blueprint for what relationships "should" look like can feel daunting, especially if you're not sure if you have ever experienced a healthy one. With alcoholic parents as our role models, we might have skewed ideas about what healthy means. Remember that there's no such thing as a perfect relationship or friendship. People are imperfect and, therefore, are bound to frustrate, annoy, or disappoint you, but you *will* find people who bring more joy than negativity to your life. Finding and recognizing this joy often involves first getting more intimate with yourself.

Before putting yourself out there to make new friends or find a romantic partner, take a self-inventory. What are your values and interests? What do you like about spending time with people? What don't you like? (This is broken down into more detailed questions in the first exercise.)

Next, mindfully put yourself in situations where making friends might come more naturally:

- Join a club, athletic group, or other social situation with like-minded people.
- Ask a friend or family member you trust if they know anyone looking for new friends or to be set up.
- Use a dating app. Many apps have friendship versions as well!
- Have a gathering at your home and ask everyone to bring one friend.

Take your friendship or relationship slowly. Remember, there is no rush to tell everything about yourself right away to see if you're a match. Part of building a relationship is doing it bit by bit. Your vulnerability is a gift, and not everyone will be deserving of it. It's healthier to get to know someone a little at time, even if it feels a little surface-level at first.

Pay attention to how your body feels. A lot of cues about danger, stress, and anxiety are stored in our shoulders, behind our eyes, and in our gut. As adult children of alcoholics, we may have grown up ignoring these cues, so it's important to do a quick check-in when you're around people to make sure they're not triggering you. You can ask yourself the following questions:

- Do I notice any sensations in my body?
- Do they feel positive, negative, or neutral?
- When did I notice this starting?

Keep a journal to log the experiences about the new people you meet. Sometimes, when we're meeting someone new, it's very exciting and overwhelming to our nervous system. We might be so focused on the other person that we forget to check in with ourselves. Often, it's not until later that our thoughts really settle and we can focus on processing our experience. (The third exercise will focus on an example of prompted journaling.)

Getting Intimate with Yourself

Identifying what makes you comfortable is the first step in laying the foundation for how you will show up in social interactions with other people. Getting to know yourself will help you provide a social blueprint of sorts for what you choose to put out into the world. Try to think of at least three answers for each question but feel free to add more if it's helpful.

What are my values? (Examples: family, career, spirituality, adventure)

....

....

....

....

What are my hobbies and interests?

_____

_____

_____

_____

When was the last time I felt comfortable and entertained in a social space? Who was I with? What were they like?

_____

_____

_____

_____

How would I describe my sense of humor?

_____

_____

_____

_____

What are deal breakers to me in any relationship or friendship? (Examples: political or religious views)

_____

_____

_____

_____

Listening to Your Body

This self-guided exercise, much like a mini meditation, will help you drop into your greatest communication tool, your body. Our bodies store memories, sensations, and feelings, all ranging from yesterday to years and years ago. Noticing what our body tells us about the people around us can help us make informed, intuitive decisions about whom we let into our circle.

There are two options for completing this meditation. You could read one small paragraph at a time, close your eyes, and reflect. Or you could read the meditation aloud to yourself using a recorder and play it back for yourself.

Think about a time when someone made you uncomfortable. It may have been a comment they made, a look they gave you, or the way they handled a situation. Take a moment, close your eyes, and reflect on that now.

Turn your attention to your body. Do you notice any changes? Do you feel a tension, tightness, pain, knot, or general feeling of unease anywhere? If the feeling could talk, what would it say?

While the feeling may not have risen from your gut, this sense of discomfort is your "gut reaction." It's a sign that you don't like something about somebody. Use this space to write notes about any feelings or discomfort that came up for you.

....

....

....

....

Journaling: New Relationships

Use these questions to prompt your journaling after meeting someone new or when getting to know someone on a deeper level. This will help keep you grounded and reflective and can also help prevent idealization or devaluation.

- What were some topics we discussed?
- How did I feel in their presence? (Examples: calm, present, distracted, annoyed, intrigued)
- What did I like about them? (Examples: physical qualities, personality qualities)
- What did I dislike about them?

- Gut check: Would I like to see them again?

_____

_____

_____

Going Deeper

Once you have decided you would like to get to know someone on a deeper level, it can be both exhilarating and scary. Here are some questions you can ask them to facilitate a deeper connection. Circle ones that you like and feel free to write more that come to mind. Keep in mind that these questions don't need to be read verbatim; you can weave them into conversation naturally. Also, consider your own answers.

Are you close with your family?

What made you want to get into your line of work?

What's your favorite part about living in this city/town/county?

Do you like to travel? Where is your favorite place to travel?

If you could have any job other than what you have now, what would it be?

When are you the happiest?

What was the hardest thing you've overcome?

What are your biggest deal breakers in a relationship/friendship?

_____

_____

_____

Building Compassion and Empathy

As children, we may have grown up trying to fix people's problems. Now that we're adults, we can witness someone telling their story with compassion but without trying to make it all better. Here are some compassionate phrases to incorporate into your vocabulary, especially when someone has told you something very sad or devastating and you're not quite sure how to react.

That must have been absolutely terrible.

Thank you for trusting me enough to share that.

I'm so sorry you had to go through that.

I can't imagine what it was like.

I am here to listen.

You can share whatever you feel comfortable sharing.

Write any of your own compassionate phrases that come to mind.

....

....

....

....

....

Healing Relationships: Pros and Cons

Sometimes, we need to take a break from certain friendships, professional relationships, or intimate partnerships because of harmful dynamics. Before jumping back into a relationship, friendship, or connection with a family member, ask yourself whether it might be in your best interest to weigh the pros and cons of reentering the relationship. This will ensure that you do not make any impulsive decisions.

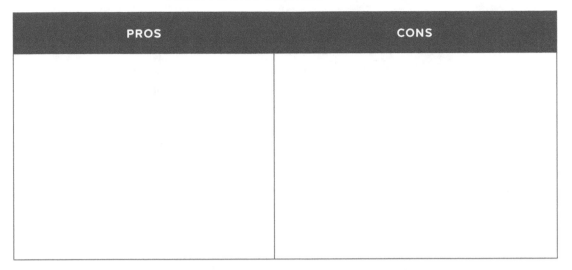

REENTERING THE RELATIONSHIP

PROS	CONS

STAYING OUT OF THE RELATIONSHIP

PROS	CONS

Identifying Red Flags

Use this list of red flags as a reference guide for when you enter a new relationship, and feel free to write down some of your own red flags or behaviors that could trigger upsetting emotions.

- Frequent insults, even if in jest
- Passive-aggression
- A sense of unfriendly or unspoken competition in the relationship

- Twisting of your words
- Yelling, screaming, or abusive language
- Learning someone has talked behind your back or violated your trust in another major way
- Invalidation (i.e., being made to feel that your struggles or suffering is not a big deal)
- Noticing you give more (emotionally or financially) in a relationship than the other person
- Jealousy about positive achievements or aspects of your life

---

Handling Conflicts

Part 1. Reflection

It's best to reflect on and communicate about conflict resolution when *not* in the midst of a conflict. This way, both parties are calm, relaxed, and able to use their rational minds. Try reflecting on these questions alone and then share them with a partner, friend, or family member as necessary.

When I feel angry, I

When I feel sad, I

When I feel stressed or overwhelmed, I

During an argument or tense conversation, I am not proud when I

I am most likely to be in a negative state of mind during these situations:

....

....

....

....

....

Part 2. Practicing

Write down some alternative behaviors or coping skills you would like to try for each scenario. (Some examples are provided as options.)

- Take a deep breath
- Ask for time-out
- Take a quick walk outside
- Splash water on my face
- Relax my shoulders and unclench my jaw
- Tell the other person exactly how I'm feeling
- Write in my journal
- Practice yoga
- Try meditation
- Talk to a loved one I trust
- Remind myself of my goals and values, such as to be kind, to stay connected to people, and to stay calm
- Cuddle a pet
- Remind myself of what I am grateful for in my life

When I feel angry, I can try ....

When I feel sad, I can try ....

When I feel stressed or overwhelmed, I can try ....

During an argument or tense conversation, I would like to try ....

These strategies could help me stay more positive overall:

....

....

....

....

Chapter Wrap-Up

In this chapter, we've learned what a healthy relationship looks like. We've explored the barriers to achieving a healthy relationship and the foundations of setting yourself up for success. Through getting to know ourselves a little better, reflecting on what we like and dislike about new relationships, and building conflict resolution skills, we reinforce the idea that connection with others is an integral part of practicing compassion, avoiding social isolation, and promoting our recovery.

CHAPTER TEN

Parenting, Caring for Others, and Being a Role Model

A great deal of parenting others involves re-parenting ourselves.

In this chapter, we'll explore what it means to parent. We'll look at the definition of a caregiver, effective and ineffective techniques, and the qualities of a healthy family. We'll explore how to go about setting yourself up for success as a parent. We'll also touch on what it means to parent ourselves. As adult children, this is an important concept because even if we do not or cannot have children in our own nuclear families, we always must be reminded to tend to our inner child during our recovery work.

Caring for Others

If you are single or partnered without children and think this chapter doesn't apply to you, resist the temptation to skip over it. Instead, pause for a moment and think about other ways you may have served as a parent figure to a child or children in your life. Are you a teacher? Nanny? Do you work in pediatrics? Do you have a niece or nephew you're very attached to or another close family friend who is a child?

Chances are, at some point, you have come into contact with a child long and frequently enough to have established some form of connection with them. Being a parent is absolutely not a prerequisite for learning something about yourself from this chapter. Most of us will hold some form of caregiver role during our lives.

Besides, we are always unearthing new ways to parent ourselves! It becomes much easier and more natural to offer compassion to others when we have regularly been practicing self-compassion. Sometimes this might look like taking a long vacation, practicing a yoga routine, or signing up for a half-marathon to motivate us; other times, when life gets chaotic, it might simply be remembering to eat three balanced meals a day and keep up with our doctor's appointments.

When we give this kind of foundational love and priority to ourselves, we are better able to recognize how to give it to others. As flight attendants always say, "Secure your own mask first before helping others!"

What Do Healthy Families Look Like?

Flora is 26 years old and the oldest of all of her siblings. Her parents divorced when she was 10 years old and when her brother, Charlie, was 6. In spite of their differences, her parents knew they had made a commitment to their children and vowed to be as supportive to one another as possible. Flora and Charlie's father moved to the next town over and remarried. He had two daughters in this new marriage, half-sisters to Flora and Charlie. Flora and Charlie alternated weeks with their parents, and their mother also eventually remarried. She and her husband adopted a baby from Taiwan.

As an adult, Flora is closest with one of her half-sisters, speaking to her every day, but she stays in touch with all of her family. The siblings all poke fun at each other and occasionally get into arguments, but as adults, they have learned to self-regulate.

Charlie developed a drinking problem in college, and after a brief family intervention initiated by his parents in which the family tearfully expressed concern, he decided to get sober. The family attended his therapy sessions until he graduated his program, and they've made the necessary changes behaviorally to support him through his sobriety.

Flora did not grow up believing divorce or addiction was shameful, because her family always openly communicated. Feelings were not treated as taboo or inconvenient, and everyone got to have a say. When Charlie was in need, the rest of the family were firm but supportive about getting him help.

You might be asking yourself, "How can I tell what's a 'normal' or 'healthy' child-parent relationship if I've never directly witnessed one myself?" This is an excellent and a very important question, which brings up earlier topics of shame and secrecy. In contrast to what happened in Flora's family, in our homes, alcoholism and other questionable or dysfunctional patterns of behavior were often overlooked, swept under the rug, and not addressed directly. This may have caused us to grow up with a very confused sense of what is "typical" and what is not, and new parents may fear inadvertently causing the same harm to their children. This fear is perfectly understandable, and it does not mean you cannot develop discretion for what are appropriate and healthy behaviors now as an adult. In fact, many young parents take what they have learned from childhood and vow not to replicate some of their parents' behaviors with their own children.

While it is important to note that cross-culturally there are different standards and norms for what is considered "healthy" or "supportive" parenting, we can point to healthy behavioral patterns of conscientious and present parents:

- Healthy parents neither suppress nor over-emote their feelings; they express and, if necessary, explain their emotions.

    - **Why is this important?** Children are often watching their parents even when parents don't realize it! They learn a lot from modeling. It's important for children to grow up without resenting, fearing, or judging their own feelings. It's also crucial to model for them what healthy expression of feelings looks like. We do not want our children to grow up believing they have to take care of us for being unable to control our emotions.

- Healthy parents follow through on consequences, punishments, and expectations to the best of their ability.

    - **Why is this important?** A child must learn the world is, for the most part, a safe and reliable place. When they experience that growing up, they're more likely to seek out trustworthy people in their inner circles. Setting a consequence and failing to enforce it is not only confusing for a child, it sets the standard that the rules don't always apply, which could have dangerous consequences of its own.

- Good parents understand they are not perfect. They actively try not to expect perfection from themselves or their children.

    - **Why is this important?** "Do as I say, not as I do" can also be confusing when it comes to perfectionism. A child watching a parent be strict or harsh on themselves may internalize that this is "normal" behavior or grow up thinking they have to hustle for their parents' love and praise. In addition, children should know it's okay to ask for help, and perfectionism doesn't always lend itself well to that.

- Healthy parents reward positive or pro-social behavior.

  - **Why is this important?** For one, positive reinforcement is an incredibly effective behavioral change agent. Negative reinforcement or punishment can be motivating as well, but it's important to keep a balance so the child's self-esteem associates positive behavior with positive feelings about themselves.

- Healthy parents give their children age-appropriate responsibilities for as long as they deem appropriate.

  - **Why is this important?** Chores and participation in other family obligations help ensure that the child understands they are part of something bigger than themselves. Family responsibilities also build mastery over time as well as a sense of mutual trust.

- Healthy parents do not violate their children's privacy.

  - **Why is this important?** Trust works both ways. Reading your teenager's journal or scrolling through their school laptop or phone (*without* reason to believe there is a safety concern) can make a child feel betrayed. If safety *is* a concern, this should be addressed directly with your child; if you feel unable to do that, seek help and support from a licensed mental health professional.

- Healthy parents clearly communicate love and affection in a variety of ways.

  - **Why is this important?** A child's nervous system needs connection, compassion, and affection in order to thrive. Saying "I love you" sincerely and often is important, but so are gifts, cards, birthday parties, and spending quality time together.

It is also important as a parent to set boundaries. These might look like:

- Ensuring you keep your personal life private; for example, do not share details about dating and/or sexual intimacy
- Avoid triangulating, or using the child as someone to vent to about other family members
- Not using the child to guilt another family member into doing something, or not putting them in the middle in another uncomfortable way
- Keeping your own mental health in check to avoid putting your child in positions where they have to take care of you; for example, frequent weeping, anxiety attacks in front of them

- Ensuring they are aware of how to speak to you appropriately; for example, using consequences for cursing, yelling, or disrespectful language
- Reminding your child that although they are their own person, you are still responsible for them for as long as they are a minor
- Having a zero-tolerance policy for physical aggression in your home

Next, we'll look at some exercises for transitioning this knowledge into actionable behavior and explore how you can brainstorm and incorporate some of your own resilience and parenting ideas.

Family Values

Here are some examples of values that may speak to you and your family. Circle the ones you'd like to prioritize. Then, in the space provided, write in any others that come to mind.

Communication

Honesty

Achievement

Emotional safety and security

Work ethic

Wealth

Diversion/fun

Spirituality

....

....

....

....

....

Take What You Like and Leave the Rest

So much of recovery is looking at what hasn't worked for us with a more critical eye, but we seldom reflect on everything that went *right*—the positive memories and experiences from our families, teachers, or communities that we may have forgotten.

Take a moment to reflect on the following questions:

- What am I grateful for about my childhood?
- If I could inherit one or two qualities from each of my parents, what would they be? Is it possible I possess those qualities already?
- What would I like to take from my childhood and give to my child?
- What would I like to leave in the past and *not* repeat?

Qualities of a Healthy Family

Check off the qualities you see in your family interactions. Keep your list as a reminder of your strengths. Write down any additional behaviors or dynamics you're proud of in your family.

☐ Family members express feelings openly.

☐ Members treat each other with respect.

- ☐ Members apologize and reconcile after an argument.
- ☐ Parents are relatively consistent with boundary setting.

- ☐ Parents praise and reward children for accomplishments and pro-social decisions.

....

....

....

Ideas for Family Bonding

Check any ideas that resonate with you for bringing together the family. Write down your own ideas as well.

- ☐ Family game night
- ☐ Family movie night
- ☐ Have each family member participate in some part of making dinner
- ☐ Family activity outdoors once or twice a month

- ☐ Ask for everyone's "peaks" and "valleys" during dinner
- ☐ No cell phones during certain family activities
- ☐ Have each parent spend one-on-one time by doing something special with each kid at least once a month

....

....

....

Setting Boundaries

After setting a boundary or punishment, we can be very hard on ourselves. The following is a quiz to see if you can pick out the most compassionate, reasonable response for you to have after your child gets upset about a boundary. (You'll find an answer key at the end.)

1. Your son got angry at his sister and threw one of his own toys at the wall, breaking the toy. Now he's demanding a new one. You:
   a. Feel bad immediately and go online to buy him a new toy
   b. Take time to collect yourself if needed, provide space for him and his sister to talk about what happened, and institute a "chores payment plan" to help him earn back money to buy a new toy
   c. Scream at him and tell him it's his fault he broke the toy so he must deal with the consequences

2. You've been frustrated recently because your partner is violating the boundaries you set with your children. For instance, your daughter got her phone taken away for two weeks because it was distracting her from homework, but your partner gave it back to her after a week. You:
   a. Take the phone away again without explanation other than "This is the way it is."
   b. Let your partner call the shots; after all, they are part of the family, too.
   c. Sit down with your partner and express your concerns about the message it sends to be inconsistent about following through on consequences.

3. Your teenage daughter has had a hard time with communicating; she often screams at you and is disrespectful. Her punishment is set to last another week but you want to reinforce her for doing so well. You:
   a. End the punishment early because you feel guilty.
   b. Tell your daughter you are proud of her for sticking it out this long and give her a big hug; tell her you have faith she will keep it up for the next week.
   c. Give her an additional punishment to make sure she really understands.

4. You follow through on boundaries, and your son continues to disrespect them even when you hold steady. You're having a hard time being compassionate with yourself. You should tell yourself:
   a. I'm a failure because what I'm doing is not working.
   b. There must be something wrong with him, and it's only going to get worse.
   c. Just because he doesn't listen to my boundary doesn't mean I'm doing anything wrong. I'll keep setting the boundary because consistency is key and I'll bring him to therapy if need be.

Answer Key:
1. B, 2. C, 3. B, 4. C

Identifying Your Personal Parenting Goals

The following are examples of some goals you may want to work on as a parent. Check the ones you'd like to work on, and feel free to write in your own examples.

☐ Spend more quality time with my partner

☐ Spend more quality time with my kids

☐ Use more positive reinforcement and less punishment

☐ Better understand my children's interests

☐ Help my kids pitch in around the house

☐ Teach my kids how to

_____

☐ Watch my tone when I'm speaking to my children

☐ Work on keeping myself calm before an important conversation

☐ Follow through on my promises

....

....

....

....

....

....

Assertiveness

As parents, especially with stubborn or refusing teenagers, it can be difficult to assert ourselves. We may feel like we're dealing with a ticking time bomb and want to handle it as delicately as possible. However, when we act and speak confidently, it shows and we're more likely to gain respect.

Assertive communication in parenting involves:

- Clear requests; no ambiguous statements
- Commands, if necessary
- Stated consequences if demands are not met
- Using your feelings (for example, saying "It makes me angry that . . .")

"Please" and "thank you" have been debated among parenting experts. Some say they are words of respect that you may want to model for your children, while others say they sometimes imply that what you're asking for is "too much" or optional. Use these words at your discretion.

Write down some examples of how to rephrase the following passive requests or statements. (The first is provided as an example.)

I would really like it if you talked to me in a nicer way. → I will not tolerate being spoken to that way, and the next time it happens, there will be consequences.

I wish you would pitch in with the chores. →

I would appreciate it if you gave yourself more time in the morning to get ready. →

What time are you going to be home from your friend's house? →

Keeping a Reinforcement Log

When we focus on what is going well in our families, we are more likely to feel grateful, see the optimistic side of things, and not harp so much on the negative. Use this log to track your progress using positive reinforcement, setting boundaries consistently, and scheduling family time. Plus, if you do this regularly, when the environment in your home starts to change, you can refer back to this chart to see if you find any patterns.

	POSITIVE REINFORCEMENT	PUNISHMENT/ BOUNDARY	HAPPY FAMILY MEMORY	NOTICED A POSITIVE CHANGE IN CHILD'S BEHAVIOR
SUNDAY				
MONDAY				
TUESDAY				
WEDNESDAY				
THURSDAY				
FRIDAY				
SATURDAY				

Chapter Wrap-Up

In this chapter, we've learned what it means to set appropriate boundaries and limits and to use positive reinforcement. We've also reflected on how some of the difficulties we may have in setting boundaries stem from our own families of origin. I hope these vignettes and exercises have further cemented the idea that what happened to you was not your fault, and now, as an adult, you can make your own healthy, happy choices for you and your family.

Conclusion:
What Recovery Means

The journey of this workbook has taken us on a winding path through the past, touched upon what we would like to work on in the present, and, finally, pointed us in the direction of our future. I hope you will see that your own strength has landed you here. We may not be able to carry everything from our past with us, but we can let it inform how we proceed.

As you continue this process, you'll find that "recovery" is not necessarily a destination, but rather a state of being. It is the way we decide to live our lives, the people we choose to let in, and the ways in which we communicate. It is continually pointing ourselves in the direction we want our lives to go, one day at a time—sometimes one moment at a time!

My hope for you is that this book has helped you start to shed the idea that you should be ashamed of who you are. Your past may be painful and confusing, but it is also the source of your resilience. What you've been through does not have to define who you are any longer—*you* get to do that!

I encourage you to continue walking confidently into the future with this new self-awareness, for although it's been a long road, it's just the beginning of your beautiful story. If it feels daunting and isolating, please reach out to a support group or a therapist (see the Resources section on page 137). Having a fellow traveler can accelerate recovery, provide some accountability, and, most important, help you feel less alone.

It has been a privilege and an honor to share your journey with you. All of the resilience you need is within you. I hope you will pick up this book again if you ever need that reminder.

Resources

Books

Adult Children of Alcoholics by Dr. Janet G. Woititz

Adult Children of Alcoholics: Alcoholic/Dysfunctional Families; "Big Red Book" used at ACOA meetings and follows a 12-step format

The Body Keeps the Score: Brain, Mind, and Body in the Healing of Trauma by Bessel van der Kolk

Daily Meditations for Calming your Anxious Mind by Jeffrey Brantley and Wendy Millstine

The Gifts of Imperfection: Let Go of Who You Think You're Supposed to Be and Embrace Who You Are by Brené Brown

Self-Compassion: The Proven Power of Being Kind to Yourself by Dr. Kristin Neff

Websites for 12-Step Meetings and Literature

Adult Children of Alcoholics (ACOA): AdultChildren.org

Al-Anon: Al-Anon.org

Co-Dependents Anonymous (CoDA): CoDA.org

Blog

Medium.com/@karaboutyourself

Mobile Apps

Calm (Meditation): Calm.com

Daylio (mood tracking): Daylio.net

Insight Timer (meditation): InsightTimer.com

Panic Relief (for assistance with panic attacks)

Finding a Therapist

Good Therapy: GoodTherapy.org

Psychology Today: PsychologyToday.com

Zencare: Zencare.co

References

Introduction

"More than 7 Million Children Live with a Parent with Alcohol Problems (2005 to 2010 NSDUH)." *CBHSQ Data.* SAMHSA.gov, April 18, 2014. SAMHSA.gov/data/report /more-7-million-children-live-parent-alcohol-problems-2005-2010-nsduh.

Chapter One: What It Means to Grow Up in an Alcoholic Home

Doyle, Glennon. *Untamed.* New York, NY: The Dial Press, 2020.

"Alcohol Use Disorder." Essay. In *Diagnostic and Statistical Manual of Mental Disorders: DSM-5.* Arlington, VA: American Psychiatric Association, 2013.

Kawamura, Kathleen Y., Randy O. Frost, and Morton G. Harmatz. "The Relationship of Perceived Parenting Styles to Perfectionism." *Personality and Individual Differences* 32, no. 2 (December 6, 2001): 317–27. doi.org/10.1016/s0191-8869(01)00026-5.

King, Keith A., Rebecca A. Vidourek, and Ashley L. Merianos. "Authoritarian Parenting and Youth Depression: Results from a National Study." *Journal of Prevention & Intervention in the Community* 44, no. 2 (March 3, 2016): 130–39. doi.org/10.1080/10852352.2016.1132870.

Simpson, Jeffry A., and W. Steven Rholes. "Adult Attachment, Stress, and Romantic Relationships." *Current Opinion in Psychology.* U.S. National Library of Medicine, February 13, 2017. NCBI.NLM.NIH.gov/pmc/articles/PMC4845754.

Chapter Two: How Has Alcohol Affected Me?

Price, M. "Genes Matter in Addiction." Monitor on Psychology. American Psychological Association, June 2008. APA.org/monitor/2008/06/genes-addict.

Chapter Three: Let Yourself Grieve

Doyle, Glennon. *Love Warrior.* New York, NY: Flatiron Books, 2017.

Chapter Four: Connect with Your Emotions and Cultivate Self-Awareness

Brown, Brené. *The Gifts of Imperfection.* New York, NY: Random House, 2020.

Linehan, Marsha, M. *DBT® Skills Training Handouts and Worksheets*, Second Edition. New York, NY: The Guilford Press, 2015.

Chapter Six: Construct Healthy Boundaries

Linehan, Marsha, M. *DBT® Skills Training Handouts and Worksheets*, Second Edition. New York, NY: The Guilford Press, 2015.
Mellody, Pia. *Facing Codependence*. New York, NY: HarperCollins, 1989.

Chapter Seven: Build Confidence and Self-Esteem

Burns, David D. *Feeling Good*. New York, NY: Harper, 1980.

Chapter Eight: Love Yourself

Brown, Brené. *The Gifts of Imperfection*. New York, NY: Random House, 2020.
Neff, Kristin. *Self-Compassion*. New York, NY: William Morrow Paperbacks, 2015.
Sincero, Jen. *You Are a Badass*. Philadelphia, PA: Running Press, 2017.

Chapter Nine: Building and Navigating Healthy Relationships

Winfrey, Oprah. *What I Know for Sure*. New York, NY: Flatiron Books, 2014.

Index

U

Uninvolved parenting, 11

V

Values, 55–57, 125
Van der Kolk, Bessel, 15
Visualization, 66

W

Weller, Francis, 59
Winfrey, Oprah, 107

Y

You Are a Badass (Sincero), 101

Acknowledgments

Thank you to everyone on the Callisto team who made this publication possible, especially Jed Bickman and Ellen Feld! I am so appreciative of the support and the opportunity to write such an important book.

About the Author

 **Kara Lissy, LCSW,** is a licensed clinical social worker and full-time psychotherapist at A Good Place Therapy and Consulting in Manhattan. She provides therapy to adult children of alcoholics, along with other clients struggling with anxiety, depression, life transitions, and relationship stress. In addition to her passion for writing, she is a two-time marathoner, an avid indoor cyclist, and a yoga enthusiast. Kara lives in New York with her fiancé, and they escape to anywhere with a beach as much as they possibly can.

Printed in the USA
CPSIA information can be obtained
at www.ICGtesting.com
CBHW082019220524
8972CB00005B/68

9 781648 768132